THE END TO END CYCLE ROUTE

About the Author

Nick Mitchell is a passionate long-distance cycle tourist, who has thousands of cycling miles to his credit and is the veteran of numerous End to Ends. He qualified as a National Standards Cycling Instructor in 2009. His comprehensive knowledge of the route, built up over many years, is to be found in this, his first cycling guidebook. Nick has previously cycled from Munich to Sheffield and Harwich to Bergen, topped off with John o' Groats to Land's End, and he recently cycled halfway round the coast of Britain. When he isn't in the office writing up cycling routes, Nick can be found out on the road guiding long-distance tours.

THE END TO END CYCLE ROUTE

LAND'S END TO JOHN O' GROATS

by Nick Mitchell

2 POLICE SQUARE, MILNTHORPE, CUMBRIA LA7 7PY
www.cicerone.co.uk

© Nick Mitchell 2012
First edition 2012
ISBN: 978 1 85284 670 1

Printed by KHL Printing, Singapore.
A catalogue record for this book is available from the British Library.
All photographs are by the author unless otherwise stated.

Acknowledgments

For Sheila Hinton of Shrewsbury

Advice to Readers

While every effort is made by our authors to ensure the accuracy of guidebooks as they go to print, changes can occur during the lifetime of an edition. If we know of any, there will be an Updates tab on this book's page on the Cicerone website (www.cicerone.co.uk), so please check before planning your trip. We also advise that you check information about such things as transport, accommodation and shops locally. Even rights of way can be altered over time. We are always grateful for information about any discrepancies between a guidebook and the facts on the ground, sent by email to info@cicerone.co.uk or by post to Cicerone, 2 Police Square, Milnthorpe LA7 7PY, United Kingdom.

Front cover: View from Pentre Hodre, near Clun (Stage 5)

CONTENTS

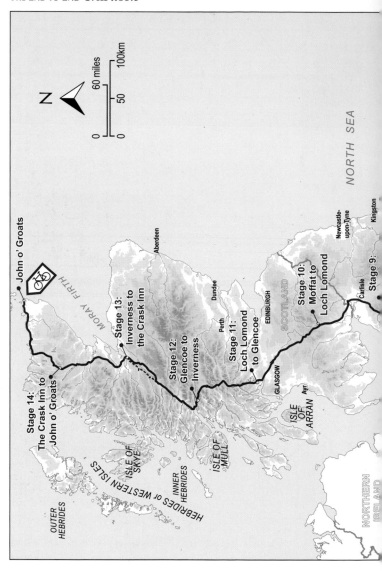

The long and winding road in the Forest of Bowland (Stage 8)
Photo: Jonathan Williams

INTRODUCTION

Cycling from Land's End to John o' Groats, or the End to End as it is popularly known, is a truly British adventure. It is a challenging long-distance bicycle tour of almost a thousand miles, from the very tip of south-west England to the far north of Scotland, usually undertaken within a two-week time frame, providing a cycling escapade par excellence. Many thousands of men and women, old and young, embark on this journey every year. The attractions of the End to End are numerous; friendship, fresh air, glorious scenery, tremendous cycling, interesting history and, upon completion, a life-enhancing sense of achievement.

Former End to Enders will evangelise with missionary zeal about their journey; the highs and the lows, the best café, the steepest hill, the longest day, the fastest descent, the calories burnt and the sun cream applied. They will tell you about the wind, the B&Bs and YHAs, road surfaces, routes, stunning views and the best pint. These are tales from the road born from practical experience, yet somewhere along the line every one of these End to Enders

The Pass of Glen Coe – one of many highlights of the trip

Stopping to fix a puncture – all part of the adventure...

will have been searching for information about how to cycle the End to End and how to put their idea into action. This guidebook is designed to give an aspiring End to Ender the tools to complete the job.

The End to End, like any other adventure worth undertaking, is also a challenge; arriving at the start line minutes before setting off will make your heart beat faster and bring a little dryness to the mouth, raising the question, 'Can I really do this?' The answer is to start and to try. The End to End is best encountered one stage at a time, one goal at a time; to get to Penzance, to the Bristol Channel, Blackburn,

Carlisle, the Borders, Inverness and head north in a life-affirming, 'I'm on my way, I've come too far and I'm not stopping.' At times and in places the End to End can be hard, but with a good level of fitness and the right preparation, it is also achievable.

Some days will be very wet, some cold, others windy. The hills can be long or steep, or both; knees will stiffen, muscles cramp, gears will click, grind and slip. There will probably be a puncture or two, but even during the tough times a smile may cross your face when the realisation sets in: 'I am cycling the End to End, I'm free and on the road and this is my adventure'.

The End to End route outlined in this guidebook is designed to take in some of the finest cycling that the UK has to offer, along the quieter A roads, B roads, lanes and cycle paths. End to Enders will find that once they are on the road, it is the numerous small and intensely enjoyable personal moments that provide the sense of adventure. The nervous tingle at the first sight of the End to End distance marker at Land's End; glimpsing Glastonbury Tor through spring morning mist; the fragrant scent of a Shropshire hedgerow after summer rain or the sound of raucous fiddle playing and laughter at an impromptu ceilidh in the Far North. On every stage of the End to End, from Cornwall to Caithness, the cycling is excellent and the landscape never really falls short of being gorgeous.

However, it is the men and women encountered along the way that add to the warp and weft of the adventure; stopping for a word with a gentleman of the road on a deserted Welsh country lane; a cup of tea with the friendliest B&B owner in Lancashire, who will talk and laugh and talk some more; arriving soaked to the skin at Slaidburn YHA and finding that the gruff-looking former Yorkshire miner, now working as a volunteer warden, will put your cycling kit in the washer with a smile. All these characters are out there waiting to take part in your End to End.

An inviting Scottish cycle path in wide open countryside

The End to End route outlined in this guidebook was originally devised for a cycle touring company and so readers can rest assured that the route and the accompanying maps and notes have been successfully road-tested by dozens of people on supported rides over the past couple of years. The brief was to design a 14-day End to End, avoiding fast and busy roads, and it has largely been met, with the exception of 8½ miles from Plymouth to Yelverton and 68 miles between Tarbet and Fort William, where there are no sensible alternatives. Fortunately on both these roads motorists are used to seeing cyclists. Wherever possible National Cycle Network (NCN) cycle paths have been used for crossing those large urban conurbations that could not be avoided.

THINGS TO SEE

From the start line in Land's End the route follows lovely peaceful lanes and charming Cornish villages and towns such as Penzance, Marazion, Praze-an-Beeble, Porkellis and Looe. Crossing the Hamoaze via the Torpoint Ferry marks the border between Cornwall and Devon, which is followed by an urban ride through Plymouth before a brilliant ascent onto Dartmoor. From Moretonhampstead the route takes in Exeter, Wells and the Somerset Levels

The coastline at Land's End

Stopping for a breather in the Far North, Sutherland

near Glastonbury before an urban stretch of cycling through Bristol into Wales via the Severn Road Bridge. From the outskirts of Chepstow there is an undulating ride through the lush wooded landscape of the Wye Valley and onwards to the relatively undiscovered, sumptuous Welsh Marches and beyond to the Cheshire Plain.

The route then continues north, taking in the rugged beauty of the Forest of Bowland to reach the splendour of the Lake District. From Keswick in the Lakes the route edges round the flank of Skiddaw to reach the historic city of Carlisle; followed by the Victorian spa town of Moffat and onwards through Larkhall and Hamilton to reach Glasgow. Cycling

through Glasgow is remarkable; a long 'traffic-free' cycle ride along the vibrant, resurgent riverscape of the River Clyde, with the Forth and Clyde Canal marking the route to Dumbarton and the remainder of the day spent cycling along the banks of the River Leven to Balloch and Loch Lomond.

With every mile forged north in Scotland the route takes on a 'big sky' feel exemplified by the stunning scenery in Glen Coe and the Great Glen. The End to End route then calls in at Inverness, the capital of the Highlands, before heading north over the Kessock Bridge to Dingwall, Bonar Bridge, Lairg and the famous Crask Inn. The route chosen here saves the best until last; the final morning is arguably the finest 32-mile cycle ride anywhere in the UK: the unsurpassable ride from the Crask Inn to Bettyhill under the shadow of Ben Klibreck before turning eastward for the last push along the coast of Caithness to John o' Groats.

On every stage of the End to End there are myriad things to see of historical, geological and other interest, and the route descriptions pick out a few highlights that are very close to the End to End route. A few exceptions require a short detour, but they are simply too good to miss – the ruins of Muchelney Abbey and Wells Cathedral, the world famous *Mappa Mundi* at Hereford Cathedral, Harrop Tarn in the Lake District and the

A striking sign in Glencoe – but not much use to End to Enders

spectacular sea cliffs at Dunnet Head in Caithness.

The natural beauty of the UK is best appreciated from a bicycle, the landscape slowly changing with each mile, and with this in mind the route was designed to traverse two National Parks (Dartmoor and the Lake District) as well as a number of Areas of Outstanding Natural Beauty (AONB) and Sites of Special Scientific Interest (SSSI).

For those riders with a keen eye there are natural highlights to be found along virtually the entire route; in the south-west, at certain times of the year, slate banked hedgerows are alive with snowdrops, primroses and foxgloves, while the Hope Valley Nature Reserve is often carpeted with bluebells. In late spring, yellow hammers and chaffinches flit and bob along the quiet lanes of Herefordshire and you may catch sight of a weasel dragging its prey across a deserted road. On the banks of the River Clyde you will probably see a heron or two, and the deafening silence of a ride through Strathnaver may only be disturbed by the crash and crump of a pheasant breaking cover.

GETTING THERE

The first issue to deal with in planning your End to End is transport to the start at Land's End. Many End to Enders rely on friends and family; for the independent cyclist, the easiest and most convenient method of

The Bodinnick chain ferry and bikes – the greenest form of transport

travelling to Cornwall is to use the train to Penzance and then cycle to your accommodation close to the start. Despite the lobbying of cycling organisations there is still a significant lack of space for bicycles on trains and this can be a real problem for End to Enders, especially during summer weekends. The simplest way to overcome this is to plan ahead and book your ticket and bicycle reservation early: seats and bicycles can be booked up to 12 weeks before the date of travel, and you should book as far in advance as possible. East Coast trains currently operate the most bicycle-friendly booking system where tickets can be bought and bicycles reserved across all train

operating companies (www.eastcoast. co.uk, Web Customer Support Team 08457 225 111, Telephone Bookings 08457 225 225; open Monday to Saturday 8.00am–8.00pm, Sunday 10.00am–8.00pm).

Penzance railway station (tel: 0845 700 0125) is at the western end of the Cornish main line, 5½ hours by train from London, and it is well served by two train companies: First Great Western (www.firstgreatwestern.co.uk; tel: 08457 000 125) and Cross Country (www.crosscountrytrains.co.uk; tel: 0844 811 0124), which both operate a comprehensive timetable of long-distance services to the station. First Great Western trains link Penzance with London, carrying a maximum of six bicycles per train, while Cross Country trains operate three daily services to Penzance, linking the south-west with Manchester, the Midlands, north-east England and Scotland, carrying a maximum of four bicycles per train.

End to Enders who arrive at Penzance railway station may wish to take advantage of a taxi journey to their accommodation near Land's End rather than the 9-mile ride. Any Time Taxis offer a 24-hour taxi service, transporting cyclists and their bicycles from Penzance to Land's End for £20 (Penzance railway station, Wharf Road; tel: 01736 888888; www.anytime-taxis.com; email: lordbuckfield@yahoo.co.uk).

Another popular way of dealing with the logistics of getting to the start of the End to End is to hire an estate car or van 'one way' down to Penzance.

Enterprise Rent-a-car (www. enterprise.co.uk; tel: 0800 800 227) have a depot approximately 5 minutes from Penzance town centre. They will also take End to Enders out to their accommodation in the Land's End area as part of their service. The depot (Longrock, TR20 8HZ; tel: 01736 332000) is open 8.00am–6.00pm Monday to Friday and 9.00am–12.00pm Saturday (closed Sunday). Hire vehicles have to be checked in personally during opening times.

Europcar (www.europcar.co.uk) also offer a 'one-way' hire service and they have a depot at Albert Street, Penzance TR18 2NG (tel: 01736 368816) open 8.00am–6.00pm

The restored watermill that is now Clun YHA

weekdays, 8.00am–1.00pm Saturday (closed Sunday).

ACCOMMODATION

Having decided upon the date of departure and selected the most convenient method of travel to Cornwall, you should consider booking accommodation as far in advance as possible; places such as Land's End, Glastonbury, Loch Lomond and John o' Groats are tourist destinations in their own right and beds may be hard to find, especially in the summer months. However, taking a quiet route through Sutherland, with some of the finest scenery in the UK, rather than the stressful A9 coastal road, comes at a price in that accommodation is limited. The reputation of the Crask Inn is growing every year; now popular with End to Enders, walkers, Munro baggers and fishermen alike, the pub is often booked up many months in advance. Luckily, if the Crask Inn is full there is alternative accommodation in Lairg and Altnaharra, which is listed in Appendix C.

GETTING BACK

Experience has shown that a firm train reservation with the accompanying bicycle reservation is an absolute necessity and it is strongly recommend to book outbound travel to Penzance and return train travel from Thurso, the nearest station to John o' Groats, at the same time. Between Monday and Saturday Scotrail (www. scotrail.co.uk) operate four trains daily for the 3½-hour journey from Thurso to Inverness, carrying a maximum of six bicycles. Sunday train services from Thurso are limited to a single train that departs Thurso at 12.22pm; with many End to Enders choosing to finish their ride on Saturday and travel back to Inverness on Sunday, competition for the six bicycle spaces on the solitary southbound train is fierce. Scotrail train staff follow company policy on bicycle carriage to the letter; if you have not reserved a space for your bicycle in advance you will not be allowed to travel.

Partly in response to the lack of bicycle space on the Thurso to Inverness train the region is now well served by an enterprising Highlander who has set up a bicycle taxi company, John o' Groats Bike Transport, which serves Inverness, Sutherland and Caithness (www. johnogroatsbiketransport.co.uk; tel: 07902 242301). The company operates throughout the year, transporting End to Enders and their bicycles back to Inverness railway station or Inverness airport. The current charge for transporting six cyclists and their bicycles from John o' Groats to Inverness is £230. If you are travelling alone you may be able to join a group who are using the taxi service; the best place to make contact with southbound travellers is at the Seaview Hotel or John o' Groats Youth Hostel.

17

Inverness – an excellent place for air, rail and bus connections

This company also offer a very handy, additional service; they have a secure bicycle drop-off point close to the finish line at John o' Groats, from which they will collect, dismantle, pack and despatch bicycles. At the time of publication they will box and courier bicycles to any location in the mainland UK for £45. They are also introducing a bicycle valet service at a small additional cost.

Travel from Inverness

Inverness is an excellent hub for transport connections to all parts of the UK. Inverness railway station is located in the city centre, with numerous local and intercity services departing daily (Station Square, Academy Street, IV2 3PY; www.nationalrail.co.uk).

Inverness Airport (www.hial.co.uk) is situated 9¼ miles to the east of the city and operates scheduled flights to London Luton, London Gatwick, Birmingham, Bristol, Southampton and Manchester. The airport is served by the JET Service 11 bus, which departs half-hourly from Inverness Bus Station (see www.stagecoachbus.com for times). Some airlines will accept properly packaged and boxed bicycles on board, but check with your carrier before booking flights.

Inverness bus station (Farraline Park, Margaret Street, IV1 1LT) is approximately two minutes' walk from Inverness railway station. The principal operators are Stagecoach, Megabus (www.megabus.com), Scottish City Link (www.citylink.co.uk)

and National Express Coaches (www. nationalexpress.com), and between them they serve most UK cities. Some bus and coach operators may accept bicycles on board if they are appropriately packaged before travelling; check with the company before booking.

Tackling the End to End from southern Cornwall to the northeastern Highlands is a pragmatic choice, as it takes advantage of the UK's prevailing south-westerly winds. However, it is also a popular route for aesthetic reasons, in that the scenery shifts from a quintessential English landscape to a far grander scale as the route moves through the Borders into the Scottish Highlands.

The End to End can be tackled at any time of year, although good weather and clear visibility will make for a far more enjoyable experience. The best period is from late March until late October, when the days are longer and warmer.

HEALTH AND SAFETY

It hardly needs stating that the most important piece of equipment for the End to End is the bicycle. It should be the correct size, well maintained and recently serviced, with particular attention paid to riding position, brakes and

Helmet and hi-vis gear are recommended – the brighter the better

gears. It will be a constant companion through the numerous highs and occasional lows of the adventure, and it is therefore important to make sure that the bicycle chosen is up to the task. The most popular choice is a touring bicycle from a manufacturer such as Dawes, Ridgeback, Koga Miyata, Trek or Raleigh, although many End to Enders complete the journey on light, thoroughbred racing cycles, rugged hybrids and even fully laden, chunky expedition tourers with 26-inch wheels.

Being visible on the bicycle and easily identified as a cyclist by other road users are two key elements of road safety that should be seriously considered by all End to Enders prior to departure. As John Franklin explains in detail in his highly recommended and excellent book *Cyclecraft*, 'to be really safe on the road, you must be seen, but you must also be seen to be a cyclist' (*Cyclecraft* is published by TSO, Norwich 2007). End to Enders should aim to be visible to other road users at all times; plan to wear light-coloured clothing for the entire journey and carry high-visibility or reflective garments that will make you conspicuous on the road in conditions of poor visibility. Additionally, always ride in the correct manner and adopt the proper road position, which will leave other road users in no doubt that they are encountering a dynamic situation involving a cyclist. It is vital that your bicycle is fitted with efficient lights and reflectors in accordance with current legislation. To read more on cycling safety and road positioning it is worth investing in *Cyclecraft*.

A distant view of Loch Ness

Helmets are a controversial issue among many cyclists and at present wearing one remains a matter of personal choice. In certain circumstances, they may alleviate the effects of a collision but they will not prevent one; there is no substitute for learning to ride a bicycle safely and confidently. If you choose to wear a helmet, then it is important to make sure that it fits correctly, that it is snug round the lower part of the forehead and that is comfortable. Additionally, a bell is a small but often neglected piece of equipment. It is a courteous method of alerting pedestrians to the presence of a bicycle approaching from the rear, which is very useful, especially on the Clyde Cycle Path through Glasgow.

TRAINING FITNESS

Successfully tackling the End to End requires drive, determination and motivation, yet mental strength alone will rarely be enough to carry off this achievement: physical preparation is equally important. If you are in any doubt about your fitness, it is worth seeing your doctor to check all is well, before getting down to the hard work of building up cycling fitness; those riders who attain a good level of fitness well before the start date tend to do very well.

The website www.doitforcharity. com has some very useful information with regard to designing a cycling training programme to suit your individual requirements. If at all possible, use the bicycle as your number one, preferred mode of transport, for commuting and shopping for example – these extra miles will pay dividends. Approximately four weeks before the start of the End to End set aside a couple of days for two consecutive long and hilly training rides of around 65 to 70 miles. This is an excellent way of checking fitness and revealing any issues with your bicycle prior to the start of the End to End.

WHAT TO TAKE

Travelling as light as possible is strongly recommended – ideally with just one pannier and a bar bag or map board. The following are essential at all times of the year:

- waterproof jacket
- waterproof overtrousers

The well-stocked phone box in Errogie (Stage 12)

Ready for the off in Cornwall

- waterproof overshoes
- trainers or cycling shoes
- cycle helmet
- cycling shorts (2)
- fleece
- cycling shirts (2)
- cycling socks (2)
- high visibility tabbard/vest
- multi tool
- puncture repair kit
- cable ties
- mobile phone
- first aid kit
- pump
- front and rear lights
- reflector
- bell
- camera
- sunglasses
- suncream
- siopel cream, excellent for saddle sores

FOOD AND DRINK

There are some excellent books on the market that deal in depth with cycling and the importance of nutrition. One particular favourite is *Serious Cycling* by Chris Carmichael and Edmund Burke (published by Human Kinetics 2002); this book is aimed at serious competitive cyclists but contains a very useful chapter with helpful tips on food choice and hydration, which is of particular relevance to End to Enders. The website www.cycle-route. com also contains a wealth of information regarding cycling nutrition.

The first step to a successful day in the saddle is to enjoy a hearty breakfast before setting out, and a big bowl of porridge with fresh fruit is a great way to start the day. Secondly, make sure that you have at least two full water bottles on your bicycle, it is crucial to drink plenty of water and replenish your water bottles throughout the day; lack of water will cause fatigue. Thirdly, buy your lunch as early in the day as possible; supermarket sandwiches and pasta meals are a cost-effective and light way of making sure that you will not be caught without food; having lunch in your pannier is definitely a case of a 'bird in the hand'.

It's best to be as self-sufficient in terms of food and water as possible. Shops, cafés and pubs can never be found when they are really needed but to help you find them should you need to, places with recommended refreshment stops (pubs, cafés, food shops) are marked on the route maps with easy-to-spot icons. It is a comforting feeling to know that you are well prepared in terms of food and water should you encounter mechanical problems or adverse weather later in the day.

	Route symbols on map extracts
∿	route
∿	alternative route
∿	detour
❯	route direction
🚲	start point
🚲	finish point
🚲	alternative finish
🔧 ☕	bike shop, café
🧺 🫖	food shop, pub

Route map scale 1:250 000 (1cm = 2.5km)
(except 1:25 000 maps on pages 68 and 129)

USING THIS GUIDE

The End to End Cycle Route is designed to be a useful resource for any cyclist planning to ride the route – from novices who want comprehensive instructions to experienced cycle tourists who are just looking for inspiration, route stats, grid refs and profiles and the latest facilities information.

You may choose to follow the described route to the letter and, if so, this guide is all that you need to take on your End to End adventure. Every left and right turn, roundabout, long ascent and sharp descent for the entire journey is described. Route maps and profiles show you what to expect every step of the way and places with refreshment stops and bike shops are marked onto the maps with easy-to-spot icons for those refuelling and bike maintenance emergencies! For every significant junction, every hamlet, village, town and city, a grid reference is provided, and all the grid refs for the main route are listed together in Appendix G, so that the coordinates for the route can be transferred to a GPS or smartphone to help you follow the route as you ride. (If you use GPX files, these are also available for each stage by going to www.cicerone.co.uk/EndtoEnd. See page 203 for full details.)

John o' Groats Youth Hostel, the last of many fine hostels along the route

Alternatively, you could use the 'bare bones' of the route, adapting it to follow either a more leisurely or a faster pace; the Route Summary Table in Appendix A, giving an overview of the 14 stages described here, and the list of the 35 Ordnance Survey maps that cover the entire route in Appendix B will help those who want to do this.

Whichever way you do the route, the accommodation information in Appendix C will be invaluable. This includes the location of youth hostels (including Youth Hostel Association, Scottish Youth Hostel Association and independent hostels), the details of at least one hotel for each stage end and a full list of bed and breakfast accommodation. Wherever possible, details of the nearest campsite are also given. In addition, the contact details or website of the appropriate tourist information centre for each leg of the journey are given in Appendix D. Finally, there is a comprehensive list of cycle repair shops in the major towns and cities along the route (Appendix E) and a handy list of cycling and accommodation apps and other relevant websites (Appendix F).

STAGE 1
Land's End to Fowey

Start	Land's End Visitor Centre (SW 345 250)
Finish	Fowey town centre (SX 125 516) or Golant YHA (SX 118 557)
Distance	64 miles (103km) or 67 miles (108km)
Grade	Hard
Time	6–7 hours
Maps	OS Landranger 203: Land's End & Isles of Scilly; OS Landranger 204: Truro & Falmouth; OS Landranger 200: Newquay & Bodmin
Refreshments	Philp's Bakery, 1 Market Place, Marazion (SW 517 307), tel: 01736 710332, Cornish pasties; Treworran Jet Garage (SW 924 423) on A3078, drinks and sandwiches; The Ship Inn, Polmear (SX 088 535) tel: 01726 812540

The first leg of the End to End may prove to be one of the most tiring of the whole adventure. There can be no doubt that the first day is a challenge; the navigation requires concentration and the cycling is demanding, particularly in the afternoon. Many End to Enders will have made their own way to Cornwall by rail or car a day or so before departure and a good night's sleep may have proved elusive. Departing from Land's End is often an emotionally charged affair and the terrain of short, sharp Cornish hills adds to the tension. In the late afternoon there is also some urban cycling through the busy town of St Austell with a final steep climb awaiting at Polmear before the easier final miles into Fowey or the youth hostel at Golant. On the other hand, the Cornish scenery is splendid, with the route chosen as far as possible using quiet lanes bordered with distinctive granite stone walls and slate-faced hedge-banks. In spring and summer these boundaries are awash with plant life; pink thrift, red valerian, white sea campion and pink and white English stonecrop all add colour to the landscape.

Before reaching the lanes of Cornwall there are some practicalities to address; for those riders who have stayed in the YHA at Letcha Vean (SW 364 305) near St Just, or in the village of St Just itself, there are an extra 5 miles and 5½ miles respectively to cycle before arriving at the End to End start line, which is situated in front of the **Land's End** visitor centre. The iconic fingerpost can be found at the rear of the Visitor Centre near Land's End Hotel.

> An interesting backdrop to the start of the End to End is provided by the **Longships Lighthouse**, which stands a mile out to sea on the Carn Bras rock. The light marks the treacherous rocks and reefs that have made this corner of south-west England a graveyard for shipping. It was built in 1875 by the Trinity House engineer Sir James Douglass and automated in 1988, before being refurbished in 2006 to utilise the latest in green technology in the form of wind, solar and battery power. The lighthouse also relies on a generator and oil-fired boiler for heating during the severe Cornish winter.

End to Enders should leave the area of Land's End (SW 345 250) Visitor Centre and cycle for 4½ miles on the A30 going through the village of Sennen, (SW 356 255) cycling past St Sennen parish church before reaching the crossroads at Crows-an-wra (SW 395 276). At the crossroads continue on the A30 for a further 4½ miles to reach the roundabout at the junction of the A3071 and the A30. At this roundabout leave the A30, taking the third exit and following signs for Penzance and Newlyn Art Gallery.

Cycle along this road for ½ mile towards Penzance (passing the Pirate Inn public house) and at the next small roundabout turn right, into Alexandra Road. Cycle onwards for a further ½ mile. At the end of Alexandra Road turn left into Western Promenade Road and continue onwards cycling into Battery Road. Arriving into **Penzance** marks the first significant town on the journey to the far north of Scotland.

As you cycle along the promenade look out for the art-deco design and triangular shape of **Jubilee Pool lido** (SW 477 298) on the right-hand side of Battery Road. This pool was designed by Captain F Latham and opened in May 1935, celebrating its 75th anniversary in May 2010.

Continue past Jubilee Pool for approximately ½ mile, cycling along the Quay and into Wharf Road. You will now need to look out carefully

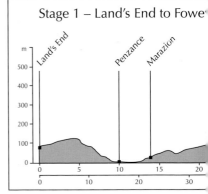

Stage 1 – Land's End to Fowey

Land's End visitor centre with cyclists ready for the off

for a National Cycle Network 3 (NCN3) sign (SW 475 305), which is mounted on the supports of a pedestrian crossing. This NCN3 sign marks an important navigational waypoint, which leads to a dedicated, traffic-free, gravel cycle path towards St Michael's Mount. Having located the NCN3 sign, it is advisable to dismount, cross over the pedestrian crossing, remount and then cycle for 360m across a large car park towards the six distinctive stands at Penzance bus station. A grey concrete wall to the right of the bus station marks the start of a four-mile traffic-free stretch of the NCN3 along the shoreline of Mounts Bay.

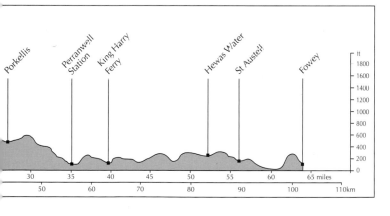

Stage 1 – Land's End to Fowey (64 miles)

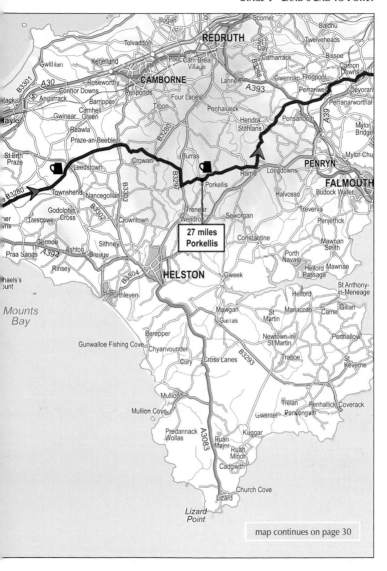

27 miles
Porkellis

map continues on page 30

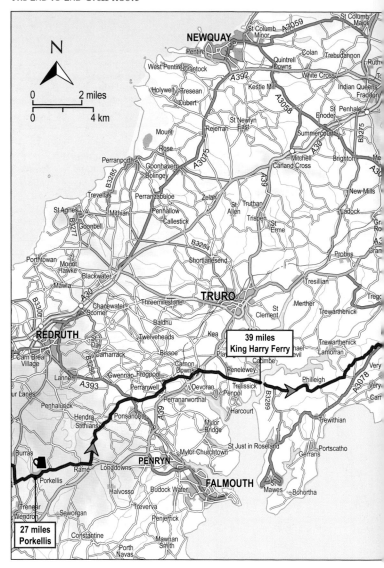

Stage 1 – Land's End to Fowey (64 miles)

The iconic St Michael's Mount – well worth a visit

The imposing outline of **St Michael's Mount** (SW 515 299) dominates the distant view. Its antecedents are that of a monastery, fortress and country house. St Michael's Mount has been associated with Christianity for hundreds of years; from as early as the eighth century there was a Celtic monastery standing on this site. On the highest part of the mount stands a 14th-century granite church, a legacy of its role as a Benedictine Priory and a sister house of the far grander Mont St Michel in France.

With the Dissolution of the Monasteries the mount fell under royal control, becoming an important fortification for defence of the south-west against the Spanish Armada. It was then used as a garrison by the Royalists in the Civil War. From 1659 the mount was held privately by the St Aubyn family before being given to the National Trust in 1954.

If time and the weather allow St Michael's Mount is well worth a visit. The castle, shops and café are open Sunday to Friday (closed Saturday) from 28 March to 31 October. Entry is £7 for adults (**www.stmichaelsmount.co.uk**).

Continue from St Michael's Mount into the village of **Marazion** (SW 517 307), which lays claim to being one of the oldest villages in England, recorded in the Domesday Book of 1086. Marazion is a convenient place to stop for a short break, **Philp's Bakery** (01736 710332, open seven days a week during the summer) at 1 Market Place, bake irresistible Cornish pasties. After enjoying a welcome breather and traditional pasty cycle through the village, ascend along Turnpike Road for about a mile to reach the roundabout (SW 534 306) at the junction with the A394. Cycle across this roundabout following signs for Goldsithney, Relubbus and Leedstown on the B3280.

Continue on the B3280 to the crossroads in Leedstown (SW 604 344). At the **Duke of Leeds** public house go straight over onto the B3280 Praze Road. Continue along this road for approximately 2 miles into the village of Praze-an-Beeble (SW 636 356). At the village crossroads go straight over, remaining on the B3280.

Continue from the village for approximately 1¾ miles to the hamlet of Blackrock. At the junction (SW 661 349) signed for Farms Common, leave the B3280 and turn right, cycling along an unclassified lane signed for Farms Common. Descend for approximately 320m and **turn left** (SW 663 347). Having turned left cycle onwards for about a mile, continuing to follow the signs for Farms Common, and at the next junction turn right (SW 678 340) onto the B3297 signed for Helston. Cycle along this road for approximately ½ mile and turn left (SW 678 330) off the B3297. This turn is marked by a distinctive sign indicating the Star Inn and Porkellis.

Having turned left cycle for 1 mile into the village of **Porkellis**, (SW 694 334) and turn left at a small junction by the **Star Inn** (www.starinnporkellis.com; tel: 01326 340237). The Star Inn was refurbished in 2010 and serves food on Friday, Saturday and Sunday lunchtimes 12.00pm–2.30pm. Continue along this quiet country lane for approximately 1½ miles into the village of Carnkie (SW 715 343). Cycle up the hill out of Carnkie and continue onwards. After about a mile look out for a 1950s-style traffic sign on a triangular traffic island (SW 727 342) and bear left at this junction following the sign for Stithians. Cycle onwards for 1¾ miles into the village of Stithians (SW 735 366). Once in Stithians go straight over the crossroads, following the sign for Perranwell. Follow this road for 1¾ miles to the junction with the A393 (SW 755 385) and go straight over. Cycle onwards for 2 miles to Perranwell station (SW 781 398). From Perranwell station cycle for a further 1½ miles into the village of **Carnon Downs** and at the far end of the village turn right (SW 800 404) into Tregye Road and follow signs for Come To Good, Point and Penpol.

Remain on Tregye Road for approximately 1¼ miles to the next junction (SW 818 399) and go straight over signed for King Harry Ferry on the B3289. Continue on this road for a further 1½ miles to the **King Harry Ferry** (SW 841 396).

The **King Harry Ferry** is one of only a handful of chain ferries in England. A rowing ferry crossing has existed at this location for over 500 years, but the current floating bridge-style chain ferry was established in 1888 and the 350-tonne vessel used today is the seventh to operate on this stretch of the

The King Harry Ferry arriving at Trelissick

River Fal. The ferry departs every 20 minutes from about 7.30am (9.00am on Sundays) to 7.30pm (9.30pm in summer), seven days a week, costs 50p for cyclists and connects St Mawes and the Roseland Peninsula with Feock, Truro and Falmouth (**www.kingharryscornwall.co.uk**; tel: 01872 862312). Occasionally the ferry hosts onboard art exhibitions and if you are lucky you may see seals in the river.

Having crossed the River Fal on the ferry, cycle onwards on the B3289 for approximately ½ mile. You will ascend a steep hill, and as the road flattens continue straight on and at a small junction (SW 851 392) follow the signs for Philleigh and Tregony.

Remain on this unclassified road for approximately 1½ miles to the village of Philleigh (SW 872 394). Cycle on from Philleigh for approximately 2½ miles to Ruan High Lanes (SW 903 399). Once at Ruan High Lanes turn left onto the A3078 and take the direction signed for Truro. After 2 miles you will cycle past JJ Harris and Sons (SW 924 423) **Treworran Jet Garage**, which is a handy place to stop for drinks and sandwiches. Continue on from the Jet Garage on the A3078 for a further 1½ miles to the village of Tregony. Turn right following the signs for Tregony Village Centre and ascend Tregony Hill. Once in the village of Tregony (SW 922 447) continue on the B3287 signed for St Austell.

After approximately 2¾ miles from Tregony turn right at a large white house called Faircross Cottage (SW 955 474), then after 160m turn left (SW 957 474) remaining on the B3287 signed for St Austell. Stay on this road (B3287) for a further 1½ miles and at the junction of the B3287 and the A390 at **Hewas Water** (SW 964 498) turn right onto the A390 cycling towards St Austell.

From Hewas Water remain on the A390 for 6 miles going into and then through **St Austell** (SX 025 521), passing Asda and Homebase. Remain on the A390 to Holmbush Road roundabout (SX 051 531) at the junction with the A3082 Par Moor Road. Turn right at this roundabout, taking the second exit, following signs for Fowey and Par.

Remain on the A3082 Par Moor Road for 2 miles and turn right following the sign for Fowey on the A3082. Go over the level crossing (SX 075 536) into Par Green and follow the road into the one-way system; look out for faint road markings indicating Fowey; take the right-hand lane and turn right onto Fastcliffe Road towards Fowey. Cycle through **Par** continuing on the A3082 and enjoy the superb sea views away to the right. Pass through the village of Polmear (SX 088 535) where the **Ship Inn** (www.theshipinnpar.com; tel: 01726 812540) is a welcoming place for one last soft drink before ascending Polmear Hill and the final 2½ miles into Fowey.

For those cyclists with a love of literature, cycle for approximately ¼ mile from the Ship Inn, along the A3082 in the direction of Fowey and turn right (SX 095 529) along a quiet lane, signed Polkerris and Menabilly. Continue along this lane for 50m and away to the right, behind a secure gate, you will see Kilmarth (SX 094 526) in the distance.

Kilmarth is one of two houses in the area formerly occupied by the novelist and playwright, Daphne du Maurier (1907–1989) who wrote numerous novels including *The Loving Spirit* (1931), *Jamaica Inn* (1936) and *Rebecca* (1938), as well as plays including *The Years Between* (1940) and *September Tide* (1948). Kilmarth was Dame Daphne's home from 1969 until her death in 1989 and the inspiration for the novel *The House on the Strand* (1969), which she dedicated to 'my predecessors at Kilmarth'.

For keen Du Maurier afficiandos her other home at Menabilly (SX 100 512), where she lived between 1943 and 1969, and which was the model for Manderley in her novel *Rebecca*, lies 1¼ miles further down the same quiet country lane used to reach Kilmarth. Du Maurier's association with Cornwall is celebrated annually at the Fowey Daphne du Maurier Festival (**www.dumaurierfestival.co.uk**), which attracts thousands of visitors from round the world.

Golant Youth Hostel

Having enjoyed a brief detour, rejoin the A3082 and turn right, continuing towards Fowey until you reach a roundabout close to the Texaco Four Turnings Garage (SX 110 525).

Alternative finish
If you are staying at the gorgeously located **Golant Youth Hostel**, turn left taking the first exit at the roundabout, and cycle along the B3269 for approximately 1½ miles before turning right (SX 104 545) towards Golant YHA; the hostel (SX 118 557) is a further 1½ miles along this quiet country lane.

If **Fowey** is your destination, turn right on the roundabout taking the third exit before cycling the remaining 1½ miles on the A3082 into the town (SX 125 516).

STAGE 2

Fowey to Moretonhampstead

Start	Bodinnick Ferry, Fowey (SX 128 521)
Finish	Moretonhampstead town centre (SX 754 860)
Distance	55 miles (89km)
Grade	Hard
Time	5½–6½ hours
Maps	OS Landranger 201: Plymouth & Launceston; OS Landranger 191: Okehampton & North Dartmoor
Refreshments	**Yelverton** (SX 521 679) Cooperative store, snacks and drinks; **Princetown** (SX 591 735) Fox Tor Café, tel: 01822 890238

The initial hours of stage two of the End to End in many ways reflect the cycling encountered on the first stage. Short, sharp, steep hills and narrow country lanes. The first hour of the journey is notable for some tricky navigation that will require concentration; however this is rewarded as the virtually traffic-free lanes provide a memorable route through the verdant Cornish landscape. Looe is the first small town to be encountered and progress onwards is marked by a steep climb up to Great Tee before flatter ground on the journey towards Torpoint. The early afternoon involves some urban cycling coupled with a short period of challenging navigation through Plymouth; there is also a section of cycling on the busy A836 to reach Yelverton. After Yelverton it is time to relax and enjoy the remaining part of the route to Moretonhampstead; this is a tremendous ride, with a tough ascent to Princetown on the quiet B3212, before a spectacular ride across Dartmoor and an exhilarating descent towards Moretonhampstead.

The start of the second day of the End to End begins on the water's edge in **Fowey**, marked by a short crossing of the River Fowey on the Bodinnick Ferry (SX 128 521). From the ferry landing in Bodinnick ascend, passing the **Old Ferry** public house on the left. Continue to follow this road for ½ mile and at the next significant junction, near Penmarlam Caravan and Camping Park, turn right (SX 135 526) and cycle on for a further ¼ mile before turning right at the telephone box (SX 138 528) following the sign for Polruan.

The water's edge in Fowey

Continue onwards for ½ mile; the road bears round to the right and descends steeply. Follow this road, then bear left going over a brook (SX 144 525) with the immaculate landscaped private gardens of Porthpean House to the left. Cycle onwards for a further ¾ mile, and at the next junction turn left following the signs for Pelynt, Polperro and Looe. Remain on this road for approximately 1¼ miles, cycling up the hill, passing the entrance to Tredudwell Manor House (SX 156 522) on the right and Carneggan Farm (SX 163 523) also on the right. Continue on from Carneggan Farm for ½ mile and at the next junction (SX 171 523) bear left and cycle on for a further ¾ mile to a house named Higher Polgassic (SX 181 525) and bear left for Looe. Cycle onwards for ½ mile and at the next significant junction called 'Longcross' (SX 185 531) turn right, following the sign for Polperro. Cycle along this lane for 1 mile to reach a junction marked by a 'sharp bend' road sign (SX 200 525); go straight ahead (the junction is also signed 'unsuitable for HGVs') and down the steep hill; **do not** follow the road round to the right. Cycle on for about a mile, descending steeply, crossing over a stream (SX 206 526) and then gently ascending. You will now be cycling through a lush, hedge-lined valley to reach a sharp right

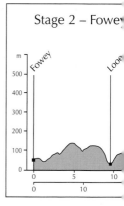

turn (SX 213 531) followed by an immediate left turn. Look for a road sign saying 'Try Your Brakes' and take this road. **Do not** cycle past the white cottage.

Continue along this lane for approximately ½ mile and then turn left onto the A387 signposted towards Looe (SX 218 533). Cycle onwards for a further 2½ miles and descend, crossing the bridge built in 1853 for the modest sum of £2980 and spanning the convergence of the East and West Looe rivers; turn left into Station Road (SX 254 536), remaining on the A387 for approximately ½ mile before turning right onto the B3253 St Martin's Road signed for Torpoint and Plymouth (SX 254 542).

> On a sunny morning the estuary at **Looe** sparkles powder blue. The town itself is essentially made up of two separate settlements: East and West Looe. It is apparent when cycling into Looe that tourism is very important for the economy of the town, while fishing is the other significant industry, with a number of fish dealers operating from the docks in East Looe. The town is also notable as the shark-fishing capital of the United Kingdom. For those with a little time to spare and wishing to savour the sights of a traditional Cornish coastal town it is worth exploring the narrow grid of streets in East Looe (to the right when crossing the bridge), which has retained its medieval pattern and is now home to numerous shops, restaurants, guest houses and pubs.

Having cycled into the B3253 St Martins Road remain on this road for approximately 3½ miles to join the A387 (SX 289 577); cycle on the A387 for a further 1¼ miles to the village of Hessenford. From Hessenford cycle onwards for 2 miles to reach the junction with the A374, then turn right following signs for Torpoint

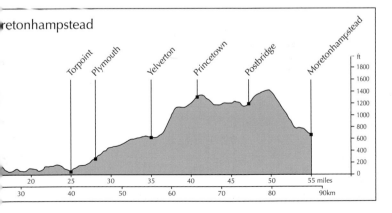

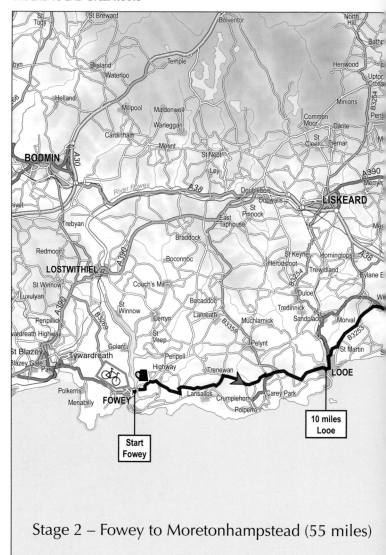

**Start
Fowey**

**10 miles
Looe**

Stage 2 – Fowey to Moretonhampstead (55 miles)

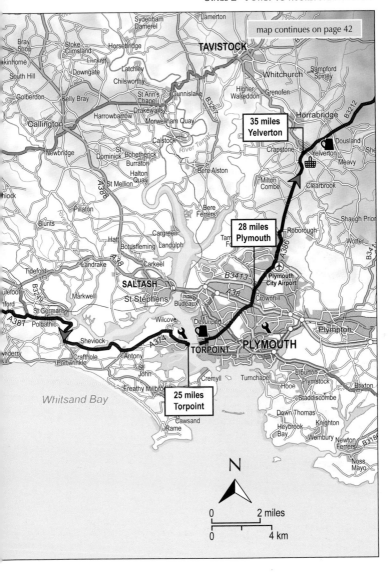

map continues on page 42

35 miles
Yelverton

28 miles
Plymouth

25 miles
Torpoint

Whitsand Bay

N

0   2 miles

0   4 km

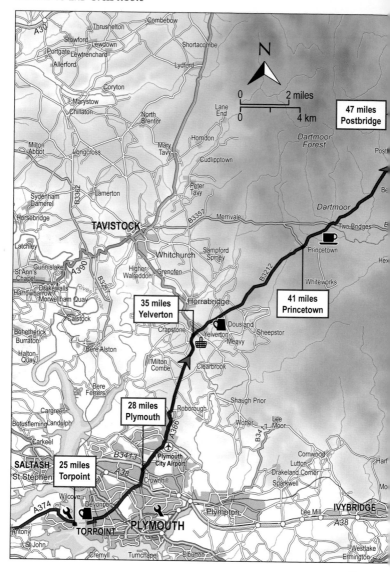

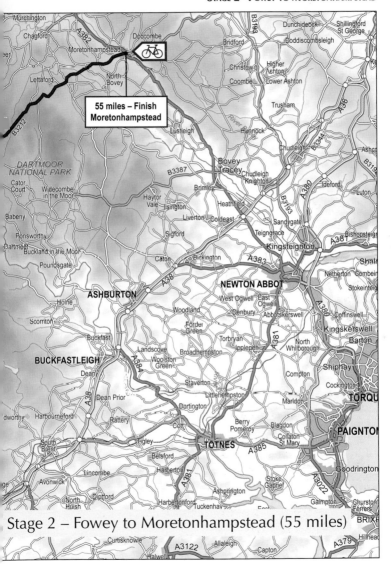

55 miles – Finish
Moretonhampstead

Stage 2 – Fowey to Moretonhampstead (55 miles)

Cyclists pouring onto the Torpoint Ferry (photo: David Anderson)

(SX 335 573). **Take care** when negotiating this junction. The next section of the End to End requires that you remain on the A374 for approximately 8¾ miles before arriving into **Torpoint** to board the Torpoint Ferry. The journey to Torpoint is notable for a tree-lined route with charming views of the River Lynher away to the left; although quite beautiful in spring and summer, the trees do make the road dark, restricting visibility for all road users. It is sensible to use lights and wear high visibility clothing on this road.

> On the final approach to the Torpoint Ferry you will notice the stark functional appearance of **HMS Raleigh** (SX 423 559). This is the Royal Navy's premier training establishment where all new recruits undertake their nine-week initial training course. In 2009/10, almost 2500 men and women who were embarking on their naval careers passed through HMS Raleigh; this establishment is also the proud home to the Royal Navy's Submarine School as well as the Defence Marine Logistics School.

Use the Torpoint Ferry (SX 441 551) (www.tamarcrossings.org.uk) to cross the Hamoaze into **Plymouth**. The ferry crossing is free for cyclists. Once across the Hamoaze, negotiate out of the ferry terminal, continue onwards for ¼ mile, cycling up the hill, going under a bridge (SX 451 552) to reach a set of traffic lights at the junction of Park Avenue. Turn left and descend for approximately 320m to the next set of traffic lights, turn right onto the B3396 Albert Road (SX 454 555) before following the signs for the A386 to Tavistock. Continue on this road for approximately ½ mile, cycling up the hill, passing the **Pheasant Pluckers Arms** public house on the left and Devonport railway station on the right. At the end of the Albert Road turn left at Stoke Methodist Church (SX 460 555) into Devonport Road, continuing onwards for approximately ½ mile where the B3396 merges with the A386 to Tavistock. The next 8½ mile stage of the End to End from Plymouth to Yelverton involves some of the most challenging traffic conditions of the entire End to End route. The cycling is made difficult as the A386 is a primary route used by numerous heavy goods vehicles and commuter traffic. The carriageway is also narrow in places.

End to Enders should remain on the A836 following the signs for Tavistock to the village of **Yelverton** (SX 521 679), which marks the end of the A836. An enjoyable afternoon now awaits. The **Cooperative store** in Yelverton is a good place to stock up with snacks and energy drinks before tackling the long ascent onto the spectacular landscape of Dartmoor.

Depart from Yelverton and cycle along B3212 Dousland Road towards Princetown, passing the **Rock Inn** (www.rockinndartmoor.co.uk; tel: 01822 852022) and Grantham Piano Services to the right. There is a long, steady 6-mile climb out of Yelverton to **Princetown** (SX 591 735). Upon arrival at the highest village on Dartmoor cycle past the Plume of Feathers Inn and continue onwards for 55m to the **Fox Tor Café** on the right (PL20 6QS; www.foxtorcafe.com; tel: 01822 890238, mobile: 07968 361977). This is a great cycle-friendly café, open Monday to Friday 9.00am to 5.00pm, with free wifi as well as a log-burning stove and open fire. The café serves all-day breakfasts, pasties, jacket potatoes, tea and coffee. This may be a very welcome stop before the final couple of hours on Dartmoor.

On the spectacular ride across Dartmoor

HM PRISON DARTMOOR

Princetown is also home to the imposing structure of the well-known prison whose origins go back as far as 1805 and the scheme of the Dartmoor land-owner, Sir Thomas Tyrwhitt, to build a gaol on the moor to house French prisoners from the Napoleonic Wars – men who were at that time being held in rotting prison hulks moored in Plymouth sound. Building the gaol took three years and by 1809 the first French prisoners of war were being housed on Dartmoor. They were later joined by Americans from the War of 1812, with both groups put to work reclaiming the barren moor for farmland as well as building roads.

With the end of hostilities against France in 1815 the prison barracks lay empty for years before being rebuilt and recommissioned as a convict gaol. Since 1850 the prison has been in constant use, and in the Victorian era it had the reputation as the toughest gaol in the country. Today the fearsome reputation has largely gone. HM Prison Dartmoor now holds category C prisoners, with work and education at the centre of attempts to rehabilitate the men. For those cyclists with a little time to spare and a passing interest in the history of crime and punishment there is an excellent museum at the prison, which is open all year round (www.dartmoor-prison.co.uk).

Leave Princetown and cycle down the steep hill on the B3212 Two Bridges Road; continue onwards for approximately 1½ miles to the next junction (SX 606 749); turn right taking the B3212 to Moretonhampstead and continue on for ¼ mile, cycling past the Two Bridges Hotel, and take the next left to Moretonhampstead on the B3212 (SX 611 750). Continue on the B3212 for approximately 3½ miles and look out for the three spans of the 14m, granite clapper bridge (SX 649 789) over the East Dart River at Postbridge on the right.

> This type of **bridge** is common on Dartmoor; originally designed for pack animals and pedestrians, it is a simple yet incredibly robust construction. This example is believed to date from the Middle Ages and is regarded as the finest example of its type on the moor.

Remain on the B3212 for a further 8½ miles from the clapper bridge into Moretonhampstead. En route to this delightful town you will pass the **Warren House Inn**, which is the highest pub in southern England at 435m above sea level (SX 674 809; www.warrenhouseinn.co.uk), and on a clear day this part of the

The medieval clapper bridge at Postbridge

ride is a tonic for the weariest of souls. There are spectacular, panoramic views of Dartmoor and the Dartmoor Forest before one final glorious descent towards the town of **Moretonhampstead** (SX 754 860).

An architectural gem awaits in Cross Street, Moretonhampstead, in the form of the outstanding **Almshouses** (SX 754 861), dating from medieval times, rebuilt around 1637 and renovated and restored in 1938. It was common practice for the wealthy to build Almshouses in Elizabethan and Stuart times, they would act as public reminders as to the charity of the benefactors. The Moretonhampstead almshouses have a thatched roof and are constructed over two storeys, featuring a stunning 11-bayed loggia, with a central entrance at ground level.

STAGE 3

Moretonhampstead to Street

Start	Moretonhampstead town centre (SX 755 860)
Finish	Street YHA (ST 481 345) or Glastonbury town centre (ST 500 390)
Distance	72 miles (116km) or 74 miles (120km)
Grade	Moderate
Time	7–8 hours
Maps	OS Landranger 192: Exeter & Sidmouth; OS Landranger 193: Taunton & Lyme Regis; OS Landranger 182: Weston-super-Mare
Refreshments	**Talaton** (SY 068 996): Talaton Inn, tel: 01404 822214) or Talaton village shop, tel: 01404 822084 (closed 1.00pm–2.00pm on weekdays); The Drewe Arms, **Broadhembury** (ST 102 048), tel: 01404 841267)

By stage three the End to End starts to take on a certain rhythm; a good night's sleep, a hearty breakfast followed by a tremendous day in the saddle. Memories of the birdsong and the thick hedgerows of the quiet Cornish lanes will be fading and today's cycling is a far easier prospect than what has gone before. Nonetheless, the immediate 1¾-mile climb out from Moretonhampstead makes for a very steep start to the day. Urban cycling follows through Exeter, with the early afternoon comprising pleasant, relaxing cycling through quiet lanes and villages. An exhilarating descent marks the route from the Blackdown Hills into Corfe, with the final miles among commuter traffic into Street and Glastonbury.

The day's ride begins by leaving the centre of **Moretonhampstead** (SX 754 860) via Cross Street with the Bell Inn to the left of the junction and Lloyds Bank to the right. You should now cycle on the B3212 for approximately 5 miles to the village of **Dunsford**. In Dunsford look out for the navigational waypoint at Briton Street Lane (SX 814 888) before cycling onwards on the B3212 for a further 5¾ miles, at which point the road passes under the A30 (SX 894 915). From this point there follows a 1½-mile ride into the centre of **Exeter**: remain on the B3212, ascend

The start point in Moretonhampstead

the short and steep Pocombe Hill, cycle along Dunsford Road, then descend to the traffic lights at the junction with Buddle Lane. At these traffic lights continue straight on into Cowick Street. Cycle along the B3212 Cowick Street, passing St Thomas parish church on the right-hand side of the road and Exeter St Thomas railway station also on the right (SX 914 919).

Remain on the B3212 to the large and busy roundabout where the A377 Alphington Street crosses the River Clyst in the centre of Exeter. Negotiate the roundabout and take the third exit, onto the B3212 Frog Street. The road then goes under New Bridge Street; continue onwards for ½ mile, and at the junction of Magdalen Street and South Street go straight over, continuing along the B3212. Cycle onwards for a further ½ mile, following the road as it bears left to the roundabout at the junction of Heavitree Road. At this roundabout take the third exit signed Broadclyst, continuing onwards along the B3212 Western Way for approximately ¼ mile to the next roundabout. At this roundabout take the third exit, cycling along the B3212 Blackboy Road (SX 928 933). Remain on the B3212 for approximately 1¾ miles, cycling past Polsloe Bridge railway station (SX 942 935) while following signs for Pinhoe and Broadclyst. At the traffic lights at the junction of Hill Barton Road and Pinhoe Road continue straight on (SX 956 938). You should now be cycling on the B3181. Continue along the B3181 for approximately 1½ miles, cycling through the village of Pinhoe (SX 964 944), and descend, crossing over the M5 (SX 974 956) before continuing on the B3181 for a further ¾ mile, then turning right (SX 984 964) following signs for Whimple, Dog Village and Community College.

A climb after Moretonhampstead

Having turned right cycle for a further ½ mile, through Dog Village, before turning left (SX 990 969) on the next left **after** Green Tree Lane. Cycle along a quiet country lane for ¼ mile to reach the **New Inn** public house, Whimple Road, Broadclyst (EX5 3BX; SX 992 972). Having passed the New Inn cycle onwards for ½ mile; at the top of a small ascent (SX 998 976), turn right signed Whimple and Higher Burrowton and continue onwards for approximately 2¾ miles before turning left by a thatched cottage (SY 041 978), following signs for Clyst St Lawrence and Talaton.

Continue on for a further ½ mile and at the next junction bear left, following the sign for Talaton. Continue along this quiet lane for 1½ miles, going over a railway bridge (SY 058 987), passing a 'Welcome to Talaton' sign,

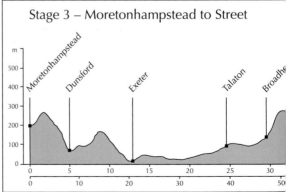

Stage 3 – Moretonhampstead to Street

continuing over a second railway bridge (SY 065 991) to Newton Corner T junction (SY 068 992) where you should turn left following the sign for Clyst Hydon.

Cycle onwards from this small junction for approximately ¼ mile into **Talaton** village (SY 068 996), which is an appropriate place to stop for lunch, either at the **Talaton Inn** (EX5 2RQ; tel: 01404 822214) or by stocking up with snacks and drinks from the **Talaton village shop** (tel: 01404 822084; closed 1.00pm–2.00pm on weekdays).

Leave Talaton with the village shop to your left and cycle up an incline for approximately ¼ mile out of the village, you should pass Woodman's Orchard on the left. At the next junction, which is signed Plymtree and Cullompton (SY 074 995), turn left. Continue onwards for approximately 2¼ miles and at Clyst William Cross Farm House (ST 072 029) turn right, signed Payhembury. Cycle along this quiet lane for approximately 1½ miles, passing Danes Mill (ST 075 034) and Egremont Farm, negotiating a sharp left turn before reaching the junction with the A373 (ST 089 037).

At the junction with the A373 go straight over, cycling for 1 mile into the village of **Broadhembury** (ST 102 048). The **Drewe Arms** is open for food until 3.00pm each day, however it is advisable to check their website for up-to-date opening times (www.thedrewearms.com; tel: 01404 841267). Having arrived in Broadhembury look for an old post box embedded in the wall of a cottage; using the post box as a reference point, turn right and continue to cycle through the village. At the Church of St Andrew (ST 102 048) take the left fork and bear left following signs for Dunkeswell and Sheldon. Cycle for ½ mile out of the village, passing Old Carriages B&B and turn right, signed Dunkeswell and Sheldon (ST 109 052). Ascend steeply for 1¼ miles through woodland (ST 116 051) and at the

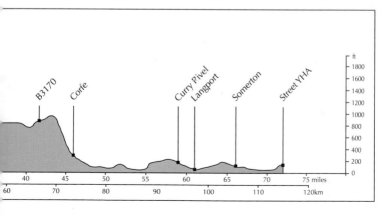

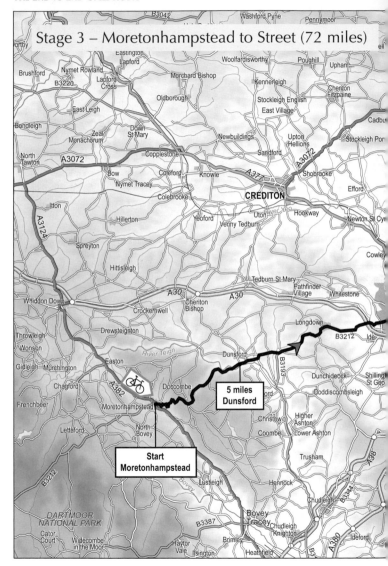

Stage 3 – Moretonhampstead to Street (72 miles)

5 miles
Dunsford

Start
Moretonhampstead

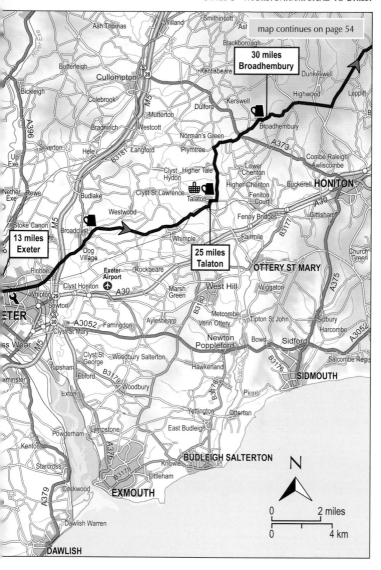

map continues on page 54

30 miles
Broadhembury

13 miles
Exeter

25 miles
Talaton

N

0   2 miles

0   4 km

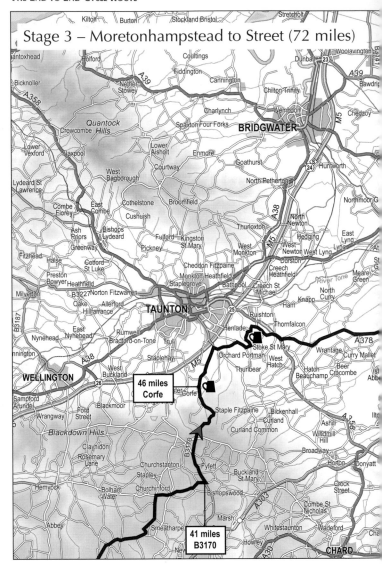

Stage 3 – Moretonhampstead to Street (72 miles)

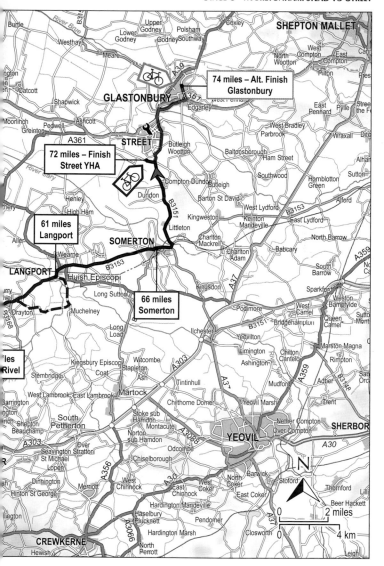

74 miles – Alt. Finish
Glastonbury

72 miles – Finish
Street YHA

61 miles
Langport

66 miles
Somerton

N

0   2 miles

0   4 km

next junction continue straight over into Long Lane. Continue along Long Lane for 1½ miles to Ewins Ash crossroads (ST 149 056) and turn left signed for Luppitt, Smeatharpe and Upottery. Continue on this road for approximately 4¾ miles into the village of Smeatharpe, passing a stock car stadium, cycling past Smeatharpe village hall (ST 197 105) and bearing left.

Cycle out of Smeatharpe on Lisieux Way; after about a mile turn right into Red Lane (ST 203 121) following the signpost for Churchinford and Chard. Cycle on for ½ mile into Churchinford and go straight over at the junction by the York Inn into Royston Road (ST 213 126). Cycle onwards for a further 1 mile, cross a stream (ST 226 130), continue for 50m and then turn left. Having turned left ascend and bear right before continuing on for ½ mile to the junction with the **B3170**, where you should now turn left (ST 235 134).

Cycle along the B3170 for 1¼ miles, and at the fork in the road (ST 228 151) bear right and remain on the B3170. Continue onwards for a further ¾ mile to Staple Hill crossroads, 299m above sea level (ST 229 163). Go straight over, following

The Half Moon Inn in Stoke St Mary

signs for Corfe. The next short section of the End to End is an exhilarating 2½-mile descent into the village of **Corfe** (ST 232 194). Once in the village go past the **White Hart Inn** (tel: 01823 421388) and continue to cycle onwards for approximately 2 miles, passing Taunton Racecourse (ST 237 215) on the right, and into the village of Shoreditch, where you should turn right into Lisieux Way (ST 242 223) signed for Orchard Portman. After approximately 160m turn left into Broughton Lane (ST 244 223); this junction is also signed as the Taunton Cycle Trail.

Cycle along Broughton Lane and after 1 mile, turn right (ST 256 227) into Stoke Road and cycle for ½ mile into Stoke St Mary (ST 264 223). You should then turn left and cycle past the **Half Moon Inn** (www.half-moon-inn.co.uk; tel: 01823 442271) and turn sharp left by the 13th-century St Mary's Church (ST 265 224).

> It is worth spending a few minutes exploring **St Mary's Church** as it contains a beautiful stained glass window, installed in 2000, the work of Patrick Reyntiens, one of Europe's finest stained glass artists.

From the Church of St Mary cycle onwards for 1 mile and at the next junction bear right and cycle along Greenway Lane for a further 1 mile to the junction with the A358 dual carriageway (ST 282 230). Thias is a very fast stretch of road and it is advisable to walk your bicycle across the dual carriageway, before turning right and cycling the remaining ½ mile up Mattocks Tree Hill to the junction with the A378 (ST 285 228). Turn left and cycle along the A378 signposted to Langport, and after approximately 4½ miles you will go through the village of Fivehead. Continue on for a further 1½ miles; on the left-hand side of the road, sitting on top of Troy Hill, is the conspicuous Burton Pynsent Monument (ST 376 252).

> The **Burton Pynsent Monument** is a 42m-high Roman-Doric style tower, complete with domed roof. It was designed in 1765 by Lancelot 'Capability' Brown and built by local builder Philip Pear at a cost of £2000. The column is now a Grade 1 listed building and was renovated in the 1990s with money from English Heritage and the John Paul Getty Trust. The Pynsent Column has an interesting history; Sir William Pynsent gifted the nearby estate of Burton Pynsent to the former prime minister, William Pitt the Elder, in recognition of Pitt's opposition to the Cider Tax. In return Pitt commissioned the construction of the column in honour of Pynsent and his generosity.

Having passed the Pynsent Column continue for another 1 mile into the village of **Curry Rivel** (ST 394 253). At this point there is a choice: continue on the A378 for 2 miles into the small town of **Langport** (ST 421 267) or take a short but hugely rewarding detour to visit the historical hamlet of Muchelney.

Detour to Muchelney

Getting to Muchelney involves a short detour from Curry Rivel. Turn right from the village into Drayton Lane (ST 395 254) and cycle for ¾ mile into the village of Drayton (ST 404 248). Pass the church and continue on for 1¾ miles, cycling along East Street and continuing into Law Lane before arriving in **Muchelney (ST 429 250)**.

MUCHELNEY

Religious life in the Middle Ages left its mark on the hamlet and the surviving collection of medieval buildings make **Muchelney** an interesting place to visit. English Heritage (www.english-heritage.org.uk) and the National Trust (www.nationaltrust.org.uk) have a firm foothold in the hamlet, with these organisations looking after Muchelney Abbey and the Priest's House respectively, reflecting the historical importance of the buildings, footings and foundations that remain.

Hundreds of years ago Muchelney, 'the great island', was a small, remote and isolated hamlet surrounded and often flooded by the wetlands of the Sedgemoor marshes. It was also home to Muchelney Abbey, the second most important religious house in Somerset. The abbey was originally founded in the first half of the eighth century, then later occupied by Benedictine Monks around AD950. The abbey was only small, relying on its more powerful sister abbey at Glastonbury for protection. The communion at Muchelney was never more than 40 strong and by the time of the Dissolution of the Monasteries in 1536 it had dwindled to only ten monks.

In the wake of the Dissolution most of the monastic buildings were demolished; today it is the surviving footings that provide a snapshot of the architectural outline of the former abbey. Close to the abbey is a splendid 15th-century parish church, and nearby is the magnificent Priest's House with its original Gothic doorway. The house was originally built by monks in 1308 as accommodation for the vicar of the parish and underwent modernisation in the 16th century.

To rejoin the End to End route after your visit, leave the village and head north for approximately 1½ miles, crossing over Bicknell's Bridge (ST 427 261), and cycle into the small town of **Langport**, turning right onto the A378 and continuing into the town to regain the main route.

From Langport, cycle along Bow Street, which then becomes North Street, and turn left at Langport Post Office (38 North Street) following the sign 'all through traffic'. Cycle past Tesco going under the railway bridge (ST 422 272) and bear sharp right before cycling along the A372 Somerton Road. Remain on the A372 for approximately ½ mile and cycle straight on taking the B3153 for approximately 4 miles through **Somerton**, crossing a railway bridge (ST 489 288) before descending Horse Mill Lane for ½ mile to the junction (ST 496 288) on the B3151 at Lodge Hill. At this junction turn left towards Street on the B3151.

Remain on the B3151, heading in a northerly direction towards Street, and after 1¼ miles pass through the village of Littleton (ST 494 305); continue on the B3151 for a further 1½ miles through the village of Compton Dundon (ST 490 327) and then cycle for a further mile, where Collard Hill (ST 485 344) awaits. This hill is usually tackled at the end of the day and is made difficult by the narrow carriageway and the commuter traffic heading to Street and Glastonbury. Nonetheless the hill is short.

At the brow of the hill turn left into Cockrod, and cycle on for 180m to reach the unique, chalet-style **Street Youth Hostel** (ST 481 345), which is set back off the road on the right.

Glastonbury finish
If Glastonbury rather than Street YHA is your chosen destination, at the brow of Collard Hill remain on the B3151 for 2 miles to Street roundabout at the junction with the A39 Westway. Cycle on the A39 for a short distance before turning right into the town of **Glastonbury** (ST 500 390), where there is plenty of accommodation to suit all budgets.

STAGE 4
Street to Monmouth

Start	Street YHA (ST 481 345)
Finish	Monmouth town centre (SO 505 129)
Distance	68 miles (109km)
Grade	Moderate
Time	6½–7½ hours
Maps	OS Landranger 172: Bristol & Bath; OS Landranger 162: Gloucester & Forest of Dean
Refreshments	Chew Stoke, Chew Valley Garage, snacks and drinks

This is one of the easier stages of the End to End. The early part of the route traverses part of the beautiful Somerset Levels on the outskirts of Glastonbury, arriving in Wells via the traffic free NCN3. Departure from the cathedral city will be memorable for the very steep 200m climb onto the Mendip Hills, which are rightly deemed an Area of Outstanding Natural Beauty (www.mendiphillsaonb.org.uk). Quiet lanes then lead towards the outskirts of Bristol where traversing the city involves a brief period of city cycling before a traffic-free ride along the cycle path that runs alongside the A4 towards Avonmouth. The area round Avonmouth can be busy with heavy goods vehicles travelling to and from the docks. The final part of the route crosses the River Severn via the spectacular Severn Road Bridge before a dramatic undulating ride alongside the course of the River Wye into Monmouth.

Having left **Street YHA** on Ivythorne Hill (BA16 OTZ; ST 481 345) rejoin the B3151, cycling for approximately 2 miles to the junction with the A39 Westway and The Causeway at Street Roundabout (ST 486 374). In the distance is the unmistakeable sight of Glastonbury Tor, now under the protection of the National Trust.

Glastonbury Tor is visibly striking for two reasons: firstly, for the 14th-century remains of St Michael's Church Tower at the summit, which was part of a collection of buildings comprising the Monastery of St Michael on the Tor, the origins of which are believed to date back as far as the ninth century; secondly, for the manner in which medieval farming altered the shape of this

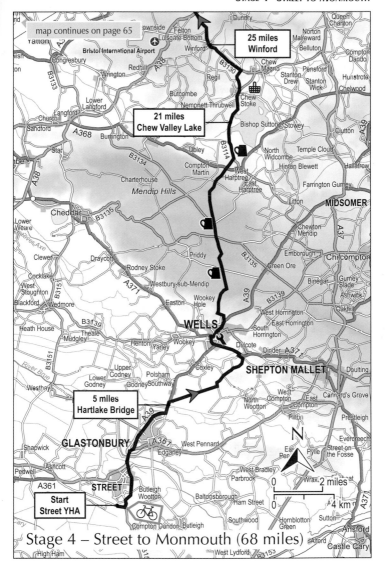

map continues on page 65

25 miles
Winford

21 miles
Chew Valley Lake

5 miles
Hartlake Bridge

Start
Street YHA

Stage 4 – Street to Monmouth (68 miles)

naturally formed hill to produce terracing, known as strip lynchets, which lie in roughly symmetrical shapes along its flanks. On a sunny, misty morning Glastonbury Tor provides a truly inspiring start to the day.

Having reached the A39 at Street Roundabout, take the second exit, following signs for Glastonbury and Shepton Mallet, and continue along this road for a further 2¾ miles to reach Tin Bridge roundabout (ST 511 406). Turn left following signs for Wells and Bath. Cycle on for approximately ½ mile on the A39 Wells Road, cross **Hartlake Bridge** (ST 514 413) and, after 140m, turn right onto the NCN3.

Take the cycle route along Long Drove, which traverses Queen's Sedge Moor (ST 525 417) for approximately 2 miles. This is a short but very beautiful stage of the End to End.

Queen's Sedge Moor forms a very small part of the 136,800-acre **Somerset Levels and Moors**. In common with many parts of the Levels, Queen's Sedge Moor comprises numerous small fields and ditches known as rhynes, which are drainage systems used to remove water from the fields so that they do not remain flooded throughout much of the year. The Levels are rich in wildlife; in summer you may see breeding birds such as yellow wagtail, sedge warbler, lapwing, curlew, redshank and snipe. In the early morning Queen's Sedge Moor is often alive with dragonflies, damselflies and butterflies. The Levels are also home to dozens of species of water beetle and make a perfect environment for wetland plants such as the frogbit, water violet, marsh horsetail and bladderwort.

While cycling along Long Drove you will go under an electricity pylon that crackles with energy; at the next T-junction turn left (ST 545 425) following the road for ½ mile to a staggered junction (ST 549 431), where you go straight over. Launcherley Hill is away to the right and an NCN3 sign stands to the right of the junction.

Cycle on for a further ½ mile, over the brow of the hill and turn right (ST

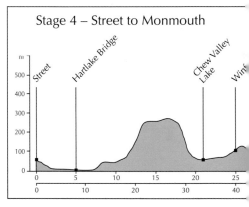

Stage 4 – Street to Monmouth

555 436) following the signs for NCN3. Continue on this narrow country lane for approximately 1¼ miles to the junction with the A371 and turn left following the signs for Wells, Shepton Mallet and NCN3. After 140m turn right, cycling under a road bridge before turning immediately left (ST 563 445), following the NCN3 along a disused railway line.

The NCN3 runs parallel to the A371 for about a mile towards the city of **Wells**. Contemporary artwork lines the cycle path. Once the path on the disused railway

line ends, the NCN3 continues alongside the A371 East Somerset Way to the roundabout at the junction with the A39 Glastonbury Road (ST 545 452). Continue straight over at the roundabout, taking the second exit onto the A39 Strawberry Way. Cycle on for a further ½ mile before turning right onto the A39 Portway. Continue along the A39 for another ½ mile and bear left onto the A39 New Street; continue on for approximately ¼ mile and turn left into Ash Lane (ST 550 464). After 60m turn right into Old Bristol Road (ST 549 464).

One example of the contemporary artwork on the cycle path near Wells

If you wish to make a short detour, **Wells Cathedral**, or the Cathedral Church of Saint Andrew (ST 552 458; **www.wellscathedral. org.uk**), is easily located in the centre of the city. This is just one of many architectural

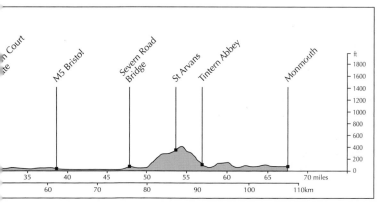

and historical gems on the End to End route. The benches that surround the lush lawns of the cathedral are a relaxing setting in which to spend half an hour before ascending onto the Mendips.

There has been a religious presence recorded at Wells as far back as AD705, but the cathedral as seen today is essentially the result of two building periods from 1180 to 1260 and 1285 to 1345. It is mainly constructed from limestone quarried at nearby Doulting, and is regarded as an exceptional example of the English Gothic style. The central gable of the west front is a masterpiece, with statues of the Apostles adorning the façade.

If you have time, take the opportunity to look inside the cathedral, where you will find one of the most impressive collections of medieval stained glass windows in the country.

Continue along Old Bristol Road, passing Mitton Manor on the left; the road then ascends steeply for 1¾ miles to 263m above sea level (ST 552 491); an aerial on top of the 305m Pen Hill indicates the summit. Continue for a further 1 mile; at the crossroads, with the **Hunters Lodge Inn** to the left (ST 550 502; tel: 01749 672275), go straight over signed for Harptree and Burrington.

Remain on the Old Bristol Road for a further 1½ miles to the Miners Arms crossroads. **Take care** at this junction; go straight over signed for Burrington B3134. Cycle along the B3134 for another ½ mile to the **Castle of Comfort** public house (ST 544 533; www.castleofcomfort.com; tel: 01761 221321), which is an important navigational waypoint. You should now leave the B3134, remaining on the Old Bristol Road, keeping a distinctive ivy-covered cottage to the left while following signs for West Harptree and Bristol. Cycle on for approximately 2½ miles from the Castle of Comfort, passing the Wellsway Inn on the left (tel: 01761 221382; Harptree Hill, West Harptree BS40 6EJ), continuing down Harptree Hill to cross over the A368 (ST 553 568) at the staggered junction. Continue straight over following the NCN3, signed for Bristol. Cycle for a further ½ mile and bear left in front of the **Blue Bowl** public house (ST 556 577; Bristol Road, West Harptree BS40 6HJ; tel: 01761 221269; www.thebluebowl.co.uk) before cycling along the B3114 with **Chew Valley Lake** on the right.

Chew Valley Lake (ST 555 594) is a lovely place to stop for lunch before venturing through Bristol. Situated at the foot of the Mendip Hills, the lake supplies much of the drinking water to the city; it is the biggest lake in the south-west and one of the largest artificial lakes in the country. Nearly 300 species of birds have been recorded at the lake, making it a well-known and internationally significant bird-watching site.

You should have no problem seeing some common residents of the lake, which include mallards, great crested grebes, great cormorants, common coots, common pochards, barn swallows and house martins, to name just a few. In addition to teeming birdlife, the lake also boasts a rich and diverse selection of plants, insects and other animals, making it both a Site of Special Scientific Interest and a Special Protection Area.

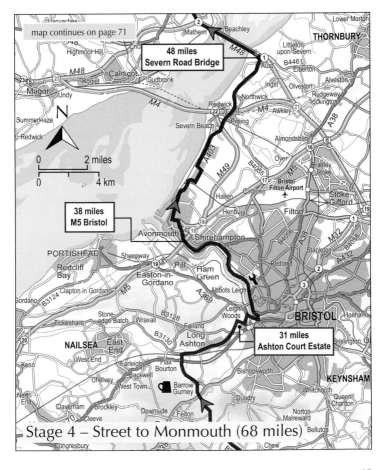

map continues on page 71

Stage 4 – Street to Monmouth (68 miles)

Remain on the B3114 for 2¾ miles from the Blue Bowl into the village of Chew Stoke, where **Chew Valley Garage** is a good place to stock up with snacks and drinks before the afternoon's ride through Bristol. Continue from the garage for ¼ mile cycling through the centre of the village before turning left into Pagan's Hill towards Winford, Dundry and Bristol (ST 562 621).

Remain on Pagan's Hill for approximately ¾ mile to the next roundabout (ST 562 634). Turn left here onto the B3130 towards the village of **Winford** (ST 542 648) and cycle along this road for 1¾ miles into the village. There is a short climb out of the village of Winford and a further 1½ miles of cycling before reaching the junction with the A38 Bridgwater Road. At the junction with the A38 (ST 533 672) go straight over into Hobbs Lane; this is signed 'no through road', but is accessible for cyclists – Hobbs Lane is also the NCN334. **Exercise caution** crossing the A38. Cycle along Hobbs Lane for ½ mile, descending into the village of Barrow Gurney. At the junction with the main road, turn left passing the **Prince's Motto** public house (ST 530 680; www.princesmotto.co.uk; tel: 01275 472 282).

Having passed the Prince's Motto pub, cycle along the B3130 for about a mile, at the next significant junction go straight ahead taking the road signed for Nailsea and Clevedon on the B3130 (ST 522 691). Cycle straight on for approximately ¼ mile, going under the A370 (ST 522 694) and up the hill to a double roundabout; at this roundabout turn right into Weston Road (ST 522 697) and continue along Weston Road for 2¼ miles into Long Ashton. Cycle through the village to the junction of Long Ashton Road and Ashton Road (B3128), looking out carefully for a sign indicating NCN334.

The gatehouse of the Ashton Court Estate – the route goes through the archway

This sign marks the start of a short stretch of traffic-free cycling and interesting navigation through **Ashton Court Estate**. Cross over the B3128 and cycle through the archway of the gate-house (ST 554 713), which leads into Ashton Court Estate; the estate has been owned for the last five decades by Bristol Council (www. ashtoncourtestate.co.uk) and is the home to the famous Bristol International Balloon Fiesta held every summer. Cycle for ½ mile into the estate, follow the cycle path to the left of Ashton Court Mansion and then round the rear of the building before turning right as the cycle path joins Kennel Lodge Road and descends for ¼ mile, passing the University of the West of England, to the junction with the A369 Clanage Road (ST 564 718).

At the junction with the A369 turn left and cycle past the Avon and Somerset Mounted Police and Dog Section building. Approximately ½ mile after turning onto Clanage Road turn right onto NCN41, signed Ashton Gate, Bedminster and City Centre. **Take care** as this turning is easy to miss. The NCN41 turning is on the elbow of a left-hand bend (ST 564 726); if you start to climb Rownham Hill you will have missed the turn. Following NCN41, go over a bridge and turn immediately right. Cycle along this traffic-free cycle path for a few hundred metres and then turn left, cycling over Ashton Avenue bridge, which is essentially an old disused railway bridge (ST 569 721); you will also see a distinctive former bonded tobacco warehouse to the rear of Ashton Avenue bridge.

Once over this former railway bridge turn left and cycle round to the front of the large Create Centre and Ecohome building. At the junction, take the signs for City Centre and Avonmouth A4. This short section of the route through **Bristol** is navigationally quite challenging; however, the objective is to cycle under the iconic Clifton Suspension Bridge away to the left. To complete this manoeuvre, once you are in front of the Create Centre and Ecohome, turn left, cycle over the dock basin in the direction of the Clifton Suspension Bridge (ST 565 732); **take care** – this part of the route, although short, is also very busy. Having reached the A4 Portway, look for and use the **cycle path** to the left of the carriageway. This is an excellent traffic-free route out of the centre of Bristol through the Avon Gorge and under the Clifton Suspension Bridge towards Avonmouth Docks.

The appearance of the magnificent 414m-long **Clifton Suspension Bridge** has remained virtually unchanged since it was first constructed in the 19th century at a cost of around £100,000. The central span between the two 26m-high piers is 214m, the deck rises to 76m above the River Avon and the bridge weighs 1620 tons (including the chains, deck structure, suspension rods and traffic). The deck of the bridge is a mere 9.5m wide and is used by hundreds of thousands of vehicles every year.

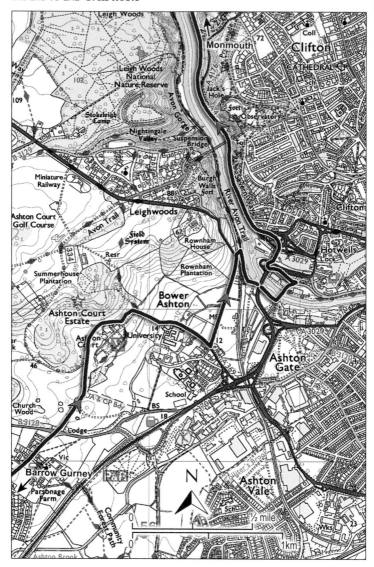

The magnificent 19th-century Clifton Suspension Bridge

The history of the bridge began with design competitions for its construction, held in 1829 and 1830. The commission to build the bridge was eventually awarded to the brilliant British civil engineer Isambard Kingdom Brunel, and the foundation stone was laid in June 1831. However, the project was beset by financial and political difficulties; it was over three decades before it was eventually completed and formally opened on 8 December 1864. Brunel himself had died five years earlier and the bridge was completed by colleagues in Brunel's honour.

Remain on the cycle path at the side of the A4 for approximately 4½ miles from the Clifton Suspension Bridge. Follow the signs for Avonmouth to the **M5 flyover**, cycle under the flyover (ST 523 773) and continue for a further ½ mile to Portway roundabout. Take the exit signed A4 Avonmouth Docks and use the cycle path at the side of Bristol Broadway, continuing to St Brendan's roundabout, where you should take the first exit signed for Avonmouth and Docks (A4).

Now continue on the A403 for approximately ¼ mile to St Andrew's Gate roundabout, taking the second exit signed for Severn Beach and Aust on the A403 (ST 516 785). Remain on the A403 for 8½ miles, cycling along St Andrew's Road, Smoke Lane, Chittening Road and Severn Road; look out for and use NCN41 as part of this journey, but **do not** continue to follow NCN41 as it eventually turns right off the A403. You will be cycling towards the Severn Road Bridge. This part of the route is busy, with numerous heavy lorries heading to and from Avonmouth Docks. Approximately 450m from the large roundabout used by vehicles to access the Severn Road Bridge turn left (ST 572 891) into Passage Road and onto NCN4. After 100m turn right by a detached cottage into Bridge Access Road and then descend to the dedicated cycle path at the side of the M48 Severn Road Bridge (ST 569 894).

Looking over to Wales along the Severn Road Bridge

Crossing the **Severn Road Bridge** (ST 560 901), opened by HM Queen Elizabeth II on 8 September 1966, is a significant milestone of the End to End, it marks the crossing from England into Wales and notably the start of a period of easier cycling. Once on the deck of the bridge it is worth stopping for photographs and to admire the engineering.

> The **Severn Road Bridge** was the first bridge in the world to use a stream-lined, aerodynamic deck and inclined hangers, and was constructed by the same collection of companies that built the Forth Road Bridge in eastern Scotland. It cost £7.9 million and took five years to build. It is also designed to withstand 100mph winds and was recently repainted to reduce the impact of thermal stress.

Use the cycle lane that runs along the left-hand side of the bridge and then descend. Follow the signs for the A466 Chepstow; remaining on the cycle path before going through a tunnel (look out for glass) and following the NCN4 signs. Negotiate Newhouse roundabout using the cycle path and look out for a Sustrans marker. Cycle along the A466 Wye Valley Link Road for 1 mile and at Highbeech round-about (ST 526 931) go straight on following the signs for Monmouth on the A466.

Continue on St Lawrence Road for a further 1 mile and at the next round-about (ST 524 945) go straight on for Tintern and Monmouth, remaining on the A466; you will pass Chepstow Racecourse on the right. There is now a steady 1¼

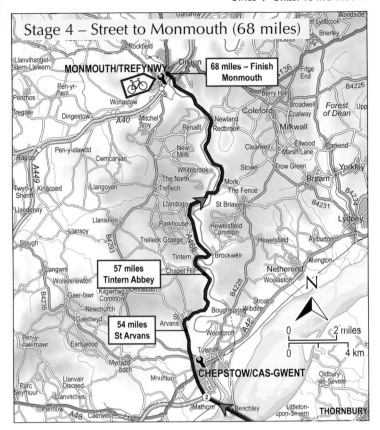

mile climb from Chepstow to the village of **St Arvans** and onwards for almost ½ mile to Lovers Leap (ST 522 968), which is followed by a superb 3-mile ride to Tintern Abbey.

After the industrial sprawl of Avonmouth Docks, cycling along the A466 from Chepstow towards Monmouth is a joy, the landscape is of lush vegetation and mature woodland with the River Wye meandering away to the right. In summer the road is sheltered and cooled by the trees and the approach to the spectacular 13th-century Gothic ruins of the church at **Tintern Abbey** (SO 533 000) marks the end of a short but exhilarating descent.

Tintern Abbey in an idyllic spot on the River Wye

Tintern Abbey was founded in the spring of 1131 by Walter fitz Richard de Clare, Lord of Chepstow, and colonised by Cistercian monks from L'Aumône in France, a daughter house of the major Cistercian monastery at Cîteaux. Tintern Abbey was dedicated to St Mary; the Cistercians sought a life of seclusion, peace and tranquillity, and lived, worked and prayed according to a strict interpretation of the Benedictine ideal. The first monks at Tintern lived in wooden buildings, but after a period of consolidation, they built a stone church and cloister. Significant rebuilding was then undertaken in the 13th century and the old Norman buildings were replaced.

In the period between 1269 and 1301 a new abbey church was constructed, the ruins of which survive to this day. The Cistercian community lived and worshipped God at Tintern Abbey for over 400 years before this was brought to a close with the Dissolution of the Monasteries in 1536. The abbey was turned over to King Henry VIII, precious metals belonging to the abbey were weighed and submitted to the king's treasury, lead was stripped from the roof, windows broken and the abbey fell into ruin.

The next 8 miles from Tintern Abbey to the village of Redbrook (SO 535 098) provide some terrific cycling; a gently undulating road with an excellent surface combine with light traffic to make the ride into Redbrook a swift yet memorable experience. From Redbrook remain on the A466 for a further 2½ miles to the junction of the A466 Redbrook Road and Staunton Road before turning left onto the A4136. Continue on the A4136 for 160m to the junction with the A40. Monmouth School lies directly ahead. Cross over the A40 and cycle into Wyebridge Street and onwards into **Monmouth** town centre (SO 508 129), where there are a number of places suitable for a night's accommodation.

STAGE 5
Monmouth to Clun

Start	Monmouth Tourist Information Centre (SO 508 129)
Finish	Clun village centre (SO 300 805)
Distance	53 miles (85km)
Grade	Easy/Moderate
Time	5–6 hours
Maps	OS Landranger 149: Hereford & Leominster; OS Landranger 137: Church Stretton & Ludlow
Refreshments	**Canon Pyon** (SO 463 488) village store, drinks and snacks; The Riverside Inn, **Aymestry** (SO 425 655), drinks and meals

This leg is the shortest of the End to End, with the route taking in some tremendous cycling through the unspoilt countryside of the Welsh Marches. The day commences with a steady climb out of Monmouth, then a short but busy stretch of the A49 into Hereford. A few miles of urban cycling through the city is followed by undulating terrain for the remainder of the afternoon, the only significant climbs being two short but very steep hills at Pentre Hodre before a sharp descent into Clun.

The Tourist Information Centre in **Monmouth** (SO 508 129) is a good place to start. With the TIC on the left, cycle to the nearby junction of the A466 and turn left (SO 510 131), taking the direction signed for Hereford. Cycle out of Monmouth, going under a footbridge linking classrooms within Haberdashers' Monmouth School for Girls, and continue to ascend on the A466 Old Hereford Road for 4½ miles to the radio mast at Llancloudy (SO 496 199). From the mast there is an exhilarating 2¾-mile descent to St Weonards (SO 495 244). Cycle through **St Weonards**, remaining on the A466 for 3¾ miles to the village of **Wormelow Tump** (SO 493 302). Continue through the village and after 1¼ miles turn left to join the A49 signed for Hereford (SO 495 324). **Caution** – this is a very busy road. To avoid any tricky navigation, you can remain on the A49 for 5 miles into the centre of Hereford.

Fortunately, there is an alternative route avoiding a large stretch of the busy A49. To take the alternative route, start by turning onto the A49 towards Hereford as in the above instructions; then after ½ mile turn left into the village of Callow (SO 495 344), go under an electricity power line and wind through

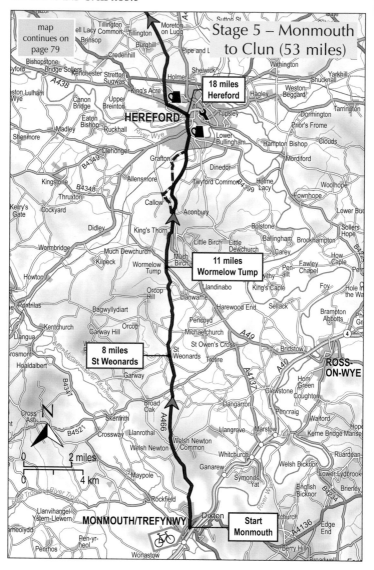

Stage 5 – Monmouth to Clun (53 miles)

map continues on page 79

18 miles Hereford

11 miles Wormelow Tump

8 miles St Weonards

Start Monmouth

MONMOUTH/TREFYNWY

ROSS-ON-WYE

HEREFORD

0   2 miles
0   4 km

Countryside at Llancloudy, near Hereford

the village for approximately ½ mile, cycling past St Michael's Church (with the church to the right), to the next T junction, where you should turn right. Cycle on for 135m, fork right and continue for ½ mile, cycling past Knockerhill Farm (SO 495 352).

At the next junction turn left (SO 498 355) and cycle along Grafton Lane for 1¾ miles, through the hamlet of Grafton (SO 496 372), before rejoining the A49 at Red Hill to the south of Hereford (SO 505 377). Having rejoined the A49 follow this road into Hereford city centre, passing the **Broadleys Inn** public house on the right-hand side of the A49. Continue into Hereford and cycle over the bridge spanning the River Wye (SO 507 395).

On the approach to **Hereford**, the magnificent structure of Hereford Cathedral (SO 513 398), or the Cathedral Church of St Mary the Virgin and St Ethelbert the King, towers over the city.

Within the cathedral is a priceless cultural artefact: the **Hereford Mappa Mundi**. It is worth taking a brief detour to examine what is the most exceptional example of a *mappa mundi* that exists in the world today. It is both a marvellous work of art and a remarkably insightful visual portrayal of life in the Middle Ages. The Mappa Mundi uses hundreds of pictures and inscriptions to depict geography and natural history as well as the spiritual life of the age. It was commissioned around 1300 by Richard of Haldingham, was produced on a single sheet of pentagon-shaped vellum and took about a year to complete. It is possible to view the Mappa Mundi, Monday to Saturday 10.00am–4.00pm (**www.herefordcathedral.org**; tel: 01432 374200). At the time of writing it is £4.50 to visit.

Having crossed the River Wye, cycle for ¼ mile, passing St Nicholas' Church on the left-hand side of the road (SO 507 398). At the next significant junction turn left (SO 507 401) into Eign Street onto the A438, signed towards Brecon and Kington. Cycle along Eign Street, then into Whitecross Road for about a mile to reach the roundabout by **The Monument** public house (SO 493 406); take the third exit signed for Knighton A4110, onto Three Elms Road. Continue along Three Elms Road for 1 mile to the next set of traffic lights (SO 490 423), where you should go straight over signed for Canon Pyon, on the A4110 Canon Pyon Road.

Continue on the A4110 for 5 miles to **Canon Pyon** (SO 463 488). The **village store** is a convenient place to buy soft drinks and snacks. Upon leaving Canon Pyon remain on the A4110 for 5½ miles, to the staggered junction (SO 440 570) of the A4110 and A44; cycle straight over following signs for Presteigne and Kingsland, while remaining on the A4110.

Continue for 4½ miles to the village of **Mortimer's Cross** (SO 425 636) and the **Mortimer's Cross Inn** (SO 425 637; tel: 01568 709212), a perfect location at which to stop and enjoy the surrounding landscape near the famous battle site.

A good late lunch stop and battle site rolled into one

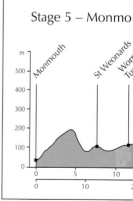

Stage 5 – Monmo

THE BATTLE OF MORTIMER'S CROSS

In the lengthy power struggle between the House of York and the House of Lancaster known as the Wars of the Roses, the **Battle of Mortimer's Cross** (SO 427 627) was an important chapter. From early morning on the 2 February 1461 the two armies jockeyed for position, with 11,000 Yorkists led by Edward, Earl of March, opposed by a smaller force of 8000 Lancastrians commanded by Jasper Tudor, the Earl of Pembroke. At midday battle commenced with an arrow storm preceding close action. The Lancastrians attacked, pushing the Yorkist right flank back to the River Lugg (opposite Mortimer's Cross Inn) and scattering them towards Ludlow and Croft Castle.

The fighting in the centre ground was a ferocious affair, with the Yorkists eventually gaining the upper hand. This time it was the turn of the Lancastrians to scatter to the west. The remaining flank of Lancastrians then tried desperately to get behind the Yorkists and encircle them, but they met with fierce resistance. The Lancastrians were finally routed and Jasper Tudor escaped, while remnants of his army were harried back to Hereford, where some of them were executed in the market square.

At the end of this historic conflict, 3800 Lancastrians lay dead on the battlefield. The Yorkist victory at the Battle of Mortimer's Cross increased Edward the Earl of March's personal prestige, hardening the will of the Yorkists to reach a final confrontation with the Lancastrians. By Wednesday 4 March 1461, just over a month after the battle, Edward, Earl of March, was acclaimed Edward IV, King of England.

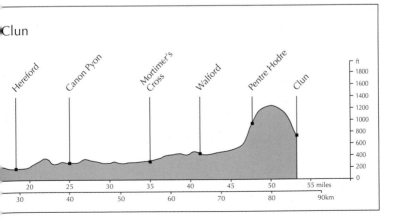

The ancient yew hedge at Brampton Bryan

Having enjoyed a snapshot of English history at Mortimer's Cross continue on the A4110 for 1¼ miles to the village of **Aymestry** (SO 425 655), where you will cross over the River Lugg. Aymestry sits on the edge of the Mortimer Forest and **The Riverside Inn** (www.theriversideinn.org) is a lovely place for lunch or just a drink.

Having crossed the River Lugg, continue on the A4110 for 2½ miles to the village of **Wigmore** (SO 414 690) and remain on the A4110 for a further 1¾ miles to the village of Adforton (SO 402 710). Cycle through Adforton and after ¼ mile turn left (SO 398 716) onto the B4530; this turning is signed for Walford, Knighton and Brampton Bryan.

Cycle along the B4530 for ¾ of a mile and turn left (SO 392 726) at **Walford** onto the A4113, signed for Knighton, and remain on this road for approximately 2¼ miles, to the junction with the B4367. At this junction turn right (SO 358 728), following the sign for Bucknell.

Cycle on the B4367 for ½ mile to a railway level crossing (SO 356 736) and then turn left, following the sign for Chapel Lawn. Cycle through the village of Bucknell (SO 355 740) and follow the road round to the right, with St Mary's Church of England School on the left. Cycle past the Church of St Mary on the right and The Willows B&B (www.willows-bucknell.co.uk; tel: 01547 530 201) on the left. Go past the **Baron at Bucknell** public house (www.baronatbucknell.co.uk; tel: 01547 530 549) and in the foreground you will see Bucknell Wood; a short distance further on a road called Seabridge Meadow is a useful navigational waypoint.

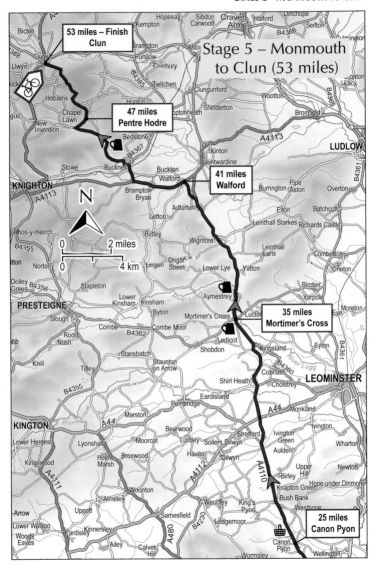

Stage 5 – Monmouth to Clun (53 miles)

53 miles – Finish Clun

47 miles Pentre Hodre

41 miles Walford

35 miles Mortimer's Cross

25 miles Canon Pyon

79

Stopping to appreciate the view from Pentre Hodre

Cycle onwards for approximately 2 miles from Bucknell, passing Quern Farm (SO 324 761) on the left. After the farm continue for 320m to a small junction, and turn right following the sign for Obley (SO 320 762). Continue up this very steep hill; as the road flattens towards the top of the hill there are exceptional panoramic views.

Cycle onwards for ¼ mile, passing a farm building with a dovecote, and take the next left turn, signed for Pentre Hodre Farm (SO 327 770). Cycle past the entrance to **Pentre Hodre** Farm, ascend steeply and continue for ¾ of a mile to the next junction. At this junction continue straight on, following the road as it ascends gently for about a mile, rounding the appropriately named Fiddlers Elbow (SO 321 786) to the crossroads (SO 315 792), where you should continue straight on following the signs for Clun.

There is now a steep ¾ of a mile descent from this crossroads; at the bottom of the hill turn left to go past the Old Farmhouse B&B (SO 311 801; www.theoldfarmhousebandb.co.uk) and continue for ½ mile before turning left into Vicarage Road. Cycle along Vicarage Road for 160m and turn right into Church Street, **Clun**. Cycle for a further ¼ mile into the village, crossing over the River Clun before finally arriving in the High Street. The White Horse public house is to the left and the Sun public house to the right. To find Clun YHA turn right along the High Street and after approximately 160m turn left into Hospital Lane and continue for ¼ mile (SO 304 812).

Clun Castle (and trusty travelling companion)

CLUN CASTLE

Clun Castle (SO 298 809) is a historical highlight of this charming Shropshire town. It is a fine example of a motte and bailey castle, and the older parts of the stonework are believed to date back to the middle part of the 12th century. It sits on top of a rocky outcrop, on a sharp bend in the River Clun, with commanding views of the surrounding countryside, including an ancient drovers' trail linking Wales and the Midlands.

The land on which the castle stands was likely to have been originally in the possession of Edric Silvaticus, also known as Edric the Wild, and then captured as part of the Norman Conquest. The castle itself was built and founded by Picot de Say, a follower of William the Conqueror. Sacked by the Welsh in 1195 and captured by King John in the Magna Carta war it then passed into the possession of Fitzalan Lords of Oswestry. It is likely that John Fitzalan was responsible for the construction of the substantial keep, which is the large tower sitting on the eastern slope of the castle mound (motte).

On becoming the earls of Arundel the Fitzalans lost interest in the castle and by 1272 it had fallen into disrepair, Owain Glyndwr attacked the castle as part of his revolt and after this the record falls silent.

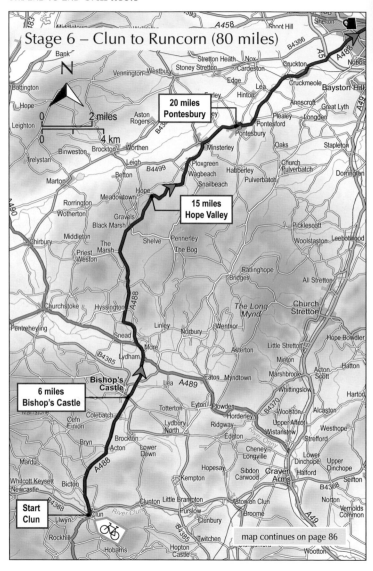

Stage 6 – Clun to Runcorn (80 miles)

20 miles
Pontesbury

15 miles
Hope Valley

6 miles
Bishop's Castle

Start
Clun

map continues on page 86

STAGE 6
Clun to Runcorn

Start	Clun village centre (SO 300 805)
Finish	Holiday Inn, Runcorn (SJ 538 796)
Distance	80 miles (129km)
Grade	Moderate
Time	8½–9 hours
Maps	OS Landranger 126: Shrewsbury & Oswestry; OS Landranger 117: Chester & Wrexham
Refreshments	The Boathouse, New Street, Shrewsbury, tel: 01743 231 658, drinks and meals; Hanmer (SJ 455 398): village store or Hanmer Arms Hotel, tel: 01948 830 532

The End to End stage from Clun to Runcorn involves an initial couple of hours ascending along the Welsh border towards Shrewsbury, with a short but spectacular ride through the Hope Valley Nature Reserve providing an early highlight as the route descends into Minsterley. From Shrewsbury onwards the route is almost flat; the main challenge is navigational rather than topographical as the route traverses through the many villages of the Cheshire Plain towards the industrial towns of the north-west. The late afternoon ride through Dunham-on-the-Hill, Helsby and Frodsham towards Runcorn can be busy with commuter traffic; particular care should be taken during the final miles of the day.

Leaving the village of **Clun** (SO 300 805), take the A488 to Bishop's Castle and cycle along this road for approximately 5½ miles. Pass through **Bishop's Castle** (SO 326 884) following signs for Shrewsbury. Remain on the A488 for a further 1¾ miles to the village of Lydham (SO 335 910). Follow the road as it bears round to the left, passing Ivy and Lily Cottages, also on the left. Continue for a further ½ mile and take the right fork signed for Shrewsbury on the A488 (SO 333 918).

The A488 then ascends for 5½ miles, rising to 311m above sea level at Black Marsh (SO 327 996); from the summit there is a superb 5¼-mile descent through the wooded **Hope Valley** towards the village of Minsterley.

Hope Valley is an 18.5-hectare nature reserve (SJ 350 016) that has been owned and managed for 30 years by the Shropshire Wildlife Trust in this quiet corner of the English countryside. In late spring the pristine woodland is carpeted with bluebells; it is also the habitat of birds such as goldcrests and treecreepers, while small mammals such as the dormouse have established themselves here.

The downhill stretch of cycling for this particular leg of the End to End effectively ends in the village of Minsterley (SJ 375 050). The rest of the stage, although long, is relatively flat. Having arrived in the village turn right at the derelict Bridge Hotel, following Station Road towards Shrewsbury on the A488. Leave Minsterley and continue for 2 miles to the village of **Pontesbury** (SJ 402 060); go through the village, remaining on the A488 for 5 miles towards Shrewsbury.

At the large roundabout (SJ 458 106) at the junction of the A488 and A5 (T), on the outskirts of the town, take the second exit into Hanwood Road (almost straight over), follow the A488 for 2¼ miles into Shrewsbury. Cycle down the hill passing the Boathouse public house in New Street (www.theboathouse-shrewsbury.co.uk; tel: 01743 231658; open daily for coffee and meals) to the junction with Copthorne Road and turn right signed for the town centre. Continue for ¼ mile to cross the River Severn at **Welsh Bridge** (SJ 489 127).

Having crossed over Welsh Bridge bear left on Smithfield Road signed for the town centre.

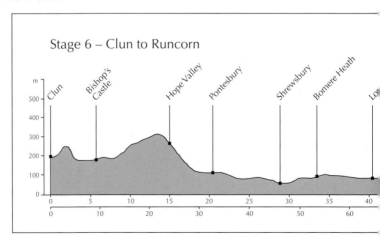

Enjoying a roadside snack at Lea Cross

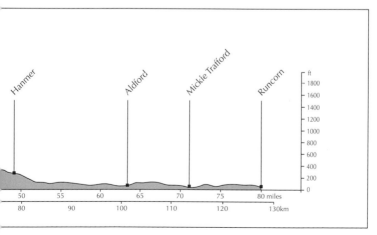

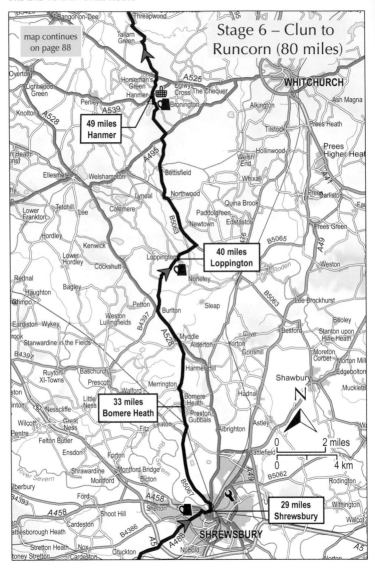

Stage 6 – Clun to Runcorn (80 miles)

map continues on page 88

49 miles
Hanmer

40 miles
Loppington

33 miles
Bomere Heath

29 miles
Shrewsbury

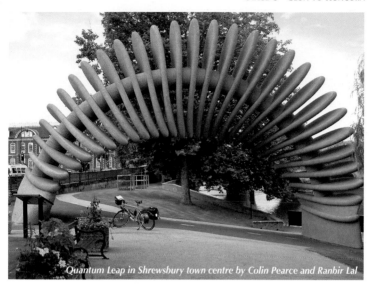

Quantum Leap in Shrewsbury town centre by Colin Pearce and Ranbir Lal

After 160m on the left-hand side of the road in Mardol Quay Gardens is the sculpture called **Quantum Leap**: a 120-tonne, 9m by 15m, £450,000 work of art honouring the life and ideas of the naturalist and scientist Charles Darwin, Shrewsbury's most famous son. The sculpture was designed by artists Colin Pearce and Ranbir Lal, evoking images of a double helix, which lies at the very core of the evolutionary process. Quantum Leap was unveiled in 2009 to mark Darwin's bicentenary (**www.discoverdarwin.co.uk**).

From Quantum Leap continue on the A5191 for ¼ mile, keeping in the left-hand lane before forking left at The Albert public house. Continue onwards for a further ¼ mile, turning left into the A528 Chester Road signed Ellesmere A528 and Telford (A5). Cycle along Chester Road and into Cotton Hill for ¼ mile before turning left onto the B5067 Berwick Road (SJ 493 135). From Berwick Road cycle out of Shrewsbury for 3 miles before turning right signed for Bomere Heath and Merrington (SJ 475 175).

Cycle on for ½ mile, going under a railway bridge (SJ 476 184), and then turn immediately left before cycling a further mile into the village of **Bomere Heath** (SJ 474 198). Cycle through the village for ¾ mile to the hamlet of Merrington, once home to the famous gardener and broadcaster Percy Thrower, before turning right (SJ 472 208) following the signs for Webscott and Myddle. This junction is distinguished by a Victorian water pump and monument erected in June 1864 in memory of Robert Aglionby Slaney, an advocate of rural and economic reform.

Follow this lane for 1½ miles to the hamlet of Webscott and turn left (SJ 475 229) signed for Myddle. Cycle along Lower Road for approximately ¾ mile to the next staggered junction (SJ 472 239) and turn left taking the A528 towards Ellesmere.

Continue on the A528 for approximately 1½ miles before turning right following signs for Loppington B4397 and Wem (B5063) (SJ 458 260). Cycle for a further 2½ miles and pass the **Dickin Arms** in **Loppington** (SJ 472 295; tel: 01939 233471).

A few yards beyond stands a neat and tidy **war memorial**, one of many that punctuate the route from Penzance to Thurso.

EDWARD UNWIN – THE PERSON BEHIND THE NAME

Behind every name on every memorial along the length of the country must be a story of sorrow, sadness, loss and tragedy. One such name, from the solitary grey granite memorial in the centre of Loppington, carved neatly into the front aspect, third from the top, is that of Sub-Lieutenant EGC Unwin, RND.

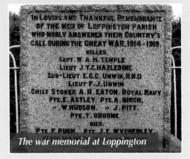
The war memorial at Loppington

This young man was the eldest son of William Unwin, the local vicar, and his wife Frances. His name was Edward. He was born on 6 January 1896 in Sheffield and educated at Orme Grammar School, Newcastle-under-Lyme. Edward was dark-haired and a strapping six feet tall. He volunteered to serve his country in November 1914 and enlisted in the Public Schools Battalion. On 4 June 1915, in the Gallipoli campaign, he was shot and wounded in the right elbow. Edward recovered from his wounds, was promoted to Sub-Lieutenant RNVR in October 1917 and served with the 63rd (RN) Division.

Just under a year later, on 3 September 1918, Edward was killed on the Western Front in France, aged a mere 22 years. He won the 1914–15 Star. Remembered forever in Loppington, this quintessential English village, his remains lie in Queant Road Cemetery, Buissy, France.

From the war memorial cycle straight on following signs for Northwood and Wem. Remain on the B4397 for 1 mile, going over the bridge that spans the River Roden (SJ 479 299). At the next significant junction turn left (SJ 484 302) signed for Northwood and Ellesmere on the B5063.

Remain on the B5063 for 2½ miles; go past the Horse and Jockey public house, continue for 320m and turn right, taking Northwood Road signed for Bettisfield (SJ 463 335). Continue into the village of Bettisfield, crossing a canal. This canal was opened in 1805 and was originally called the Ellesmere Canal, before being absorbed into the Shropshire Union Canal network and finally renamed the Llangollen Canal.

Carry on from the Llangollen Canal for approximately a mile, passing St John the Baptist church on the left (SJ 462 361), to the junction with the A495; then turn right (SJ 462 372) following the sign for the A495 to Whitchurch. Continue for ¼ mile, turn left into New Road taking the road signed to Arowry and Hanmer (SJ 464 375). Cycle along this road and after 1¼ miles follow the road signs for Hanmer and Penley. Cycle on, passing a telephone box on the right-hand side of the road before descending into the village of **Hanmer** and then bearing sharp right.

Cycle past **Hanmer Village Stores** on the right and then **The Hanmer Arms** Hotel (www.hanmerarms.co.uk; tel: 01948 830 532) on the left (SJ 455 398). Continue along this road, passing a Flare garage on the right then cycling on for 160m to the junction with the A539; turn right here, then after 60m turn immediately left (SJ 455 401), following signs for for Little Arowry and Horseman's Green; cycle on for approximately ¾ mile to the junction with the A525.

At this junction (SJ 458 413) go straight over signed for Willington and Tallarn Green, cycle onwards for approximately 1½ miles before turning right into the village of Tallarn Green. After another ¼ mile go left at the junction following signs for Tallarn Green and Threapwood. Follow the road through Tallarn Green and after a mile go over Sarn Bridge (SJ 440 448), continuing into the village of Threapwood (SJ 439 455).

Cycle through Threapwood and after ¼ mile turn left onto the B5069 Wrexham Road, following signs for Bangor. After ¼ mile fork right (SJ 435 465), now following signs for Shocklach and Farndon. Remain on this road for 1¾ miles into the village of Shocklach (SJ 438 492), passing the Bull public house on the right before cycling onwards for a further 3¼ miles to the junction with the A534 (SJ 422 540). At this junction go straight over following signs for the B5130 to Chester. Remain on the B5130 for 3 miles to the village of **Aldford** (SJ 423 595); look out for the **Grosvenor Arms** public house as a navigational waypoint and from there keep going for approximately 100m; cycle over the bridge spanning Aldford Brook then turn immediately right into Chapel Lane, following road signs for Bruera and Saighton.

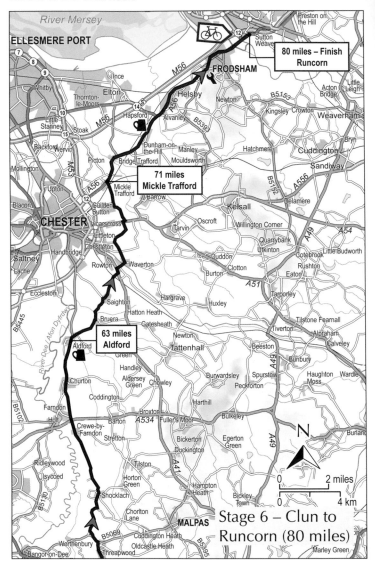

Stage 6 – Clun to Runcorn (80 miles)

Remain on Chapel Lane for 1¼ miles to the hamlet of Bruera and look out for the church on the right-hand side of the road (SJ 437 606). A Grade II listed Norman church, St Mary's is notable for its striking slender spire and shingled bell-turret, which were built in 1896 when the church was restored for the Duke of Westminster by WM Boden.

Continue along Chapel Lane for a further 1 mile to the village of **Saighton**. Keep Abbey Gate College, Saighton (SJ 442 618), to the right and then turn right by a red sandstone water tower (built around 1870) and cycle towards Waverton along Saighton Lane. Remain on Saighton Lane for 1½ miles to the A41 (SJ 453 638) and turn left towards Chester; after 120m turn right (SJ 452 640) into Eggbridge Lane, following signs for Tarvin, Tarporley, Crocky Trail and Walk Mill.

Now cycle along Eggbridge Lane for approximately ½ mile, going over the canal, and turn left into Brown Heath Road (SJ 457 644). Cycle along Brown Heath Road for a further ½ mile; at the crossroads go straight over following signs for Tarvin, Northwich; remain on this road for a further 1½ miles, passing Birch Bank Farm to reach the junction with the A51 Tarvin Road (SJ 456 671). Turn right at the A51 T junction and cycle on for 120m before turning immediately left into Wicker Lane, signed for Guilden Sutton and Mickle Trafford; follow this road for 1 mile. At Guilden Sutton Methodist Chapel continue straight on (SJ 450 684). Cycle on for a further 1 mile, going through two railway arches to reach the A56 at **Mickle Trafford**. This navigationally important junction is signed left for Chester and right for Warrington. **Turn right** onto the A56 (SJ 445 696) and keep going, following signs for Manchester, Warrington, Helsby and Frodsham.

Cycle on the A56 Warrington Road for 2¾ miles to the **Dunham Arms** public house (SJ 474 731), and then keep going for a further 1 mile to the T junction with the A5117; at this junction turn right signed for Helsby and Frodsham, remaining on the A56. Cycle along the A56 for another 1 mile through the town of Helsby (SJ 488 757) and continue on for a further 2½ miles into the town of Frodsham (SJ 517 779), where you will pass the Bears Paw public house on the left.

This Cheshire town offers B&B accommodation, a list of which can be found in Appendix C. However, to press on a little further, ascend the gentle hill out of Frodsham and continue on the A56 for 1¼ miles, crossing the River Weaver (SJ 530 785) and then the Weaver Navigation (SJ 535 789). Continue from the Weaver Navigation for ½ mile and turn left into Wood Lane, following this road for ¼ mile to the Holiday Inn, **Runcorn** (SJ 538 796), an excellent and reasonably priced hotel in which to spend the night.

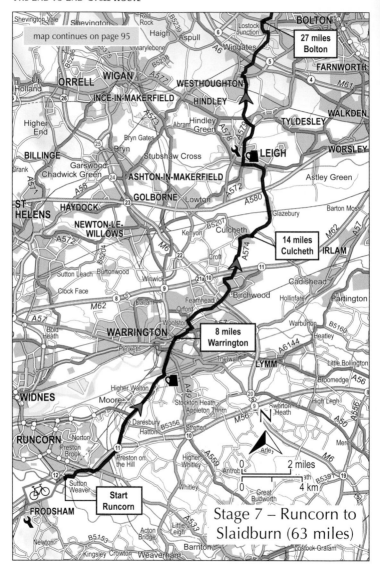

map continues on page 95

27 miles
Bolton

14 miles
Culcheth

8 miles
Warrington

Start
Runcorn

Stage 7 – Runcorn to
Slaidburn (63 miles)

STAGE 7
Runcorn to Slaidburn

Start	Holiday Inn, Runcorn (SJ 538 796)
Finish	Hark to Bounty public house, Slaidburn (SD 712 524)
Distance	63 miles (101km)
Grade	Moderate/Hard
Time	6½–7½ hours
Maps	OS Landranger 108: Liverpool; OS Landranger 109: Manchester; OS Landranger 103: Blackburn & Burnley
Refreshments	The Black Dog, 2–6 Church Street, **Belmont** (SD 674 163), meals and drinks

After the relatively easy cycling of the Cheshire Plain this leg marks a return to urban cycling and tougher terrain; the early part of the day is spent navigating through Warrington, Leigh, Atherton, Westhoughton and Bolton. You then ascend to Tockholes before descending and tackling some challenging navigation through Blackburn, which is the last major conurbation before the final miles of the stage, through the sumptuous scenery of the Forest of Bowland and onwards to Slaidburn.

From your accommodation in Helsby, Frodsham or **Runcorn** it is important to rejoin the A56 and head east in the direction of Warrington. Continue to the roundabout at Junction 11 of the M56 (SJ 574 814); **take care** negotiating this busy junction and remain on the A56 Chester Road for 3½ miles following the signs for the A5060 to Warrington. Cycle on and bear left by the **Stag Inn** (SJ 605 861); cycle over an iron bridge (SJ 604 862), continue for 1 mile and at the next roundabout, with St James's Church (SJ 607 876) on the right, take the second exit onto Wilderspool Causeway and on towards **Warrington** town centre. Keep going for ¼ mile and at the next roundabout (SJ 608 879) take the third exit into Mersey Street, signed for Wigan A49, Irlam (A57) and Motorway M62.

Cycle onwards for ¼ mile to the next roundabout, go straight over into Fennel Street and follow the signs for Wigan A49, Irlam (A57). Continue on Fennel Street for ¼ mile to Cockhedge Green roundabout (SJ 612 886) and take the fourth exit into Manchester Road, signed for Irlam A57, Birmingham (M6).

Cycle along Manchester Road for ¾ mile and at the junction close to Bruche Cemetery turn left (SJ 625 891), signed for Wigan A50 and Preston (M6). Continue on this road for a further ½ mile and turn right into Birchwood Way on the A574 (SJ 620 898), signed for Leigh and Manchester. Cycle along Birchwood Way for 1½ miles to a roundabout and go straight on following signs for Risley and Birchwood. Birchwood Way then crosses the M6 (SJ 643 910) and after a further ½ mile turn left onto the A574 signed for Leigh (SJ 649 917).

Keep following the A574 towards Leigh and after about a mile this road goes over the M62 (SJ 651 930). After a further ¼ mile the End to End route passes HM Prison Service Risley on the right (SJ 652 936). This is a catergory C male training prison that houses around 1065 inmates.

From the prison cycle on for a further 1 mile into the village of **Culcheth** (SJ 656 953) and continue through the village for 2¾ miles on the A574 to the roundabout at the junction of the A580 Liverpool–Manchester, East Lancs Road (SJ 669 983). Go straight over and continue on the A574 Warrington Road for ¾ miles; go over the bridge that spans the Leeds and Liverpool Canal and then turn immediately left onto the A572 signed Town Centre, Wigan and Bolton (SJ 670 996).

Cycle on for a further 1 mile and at **The Goose** public house and Leigh bus station turn right onto the B5215 King Street (SD 657 000) and the NCN86. Cycle along this road for approximately 1¾ miles and turn left into Lovers Lane, signed for Westhoughton B5235 (SD 664 024).

Continue along the B5235 for ¼ mile and cross the junction with the A579 Atherleigh Way. Cycle on for a further ½ mile and cross the junction with the A577 Wigan Road (SD 659 030). Remain on the B5235 for a further 1½ miles to the junction with A58 Cricketers Way (SD 657 057); turn left and cycle on for 160m, then turn right (SD 655 057) onto the B5235, Mill Street.

Cycle on for ¾ mile along Mill Street and into Bolton Road to reach the A6 Manchester Road (SD 663 066). Go straight over into Bolton Road following signs for Lostock and Chew Moor.

Cycle along Bolton Road for 100m and at a mini roundabout **bear left** into Chew Moor Lane signed for Lostock. Cycle on for a further 1½ miles to

A fountain in Belmont village

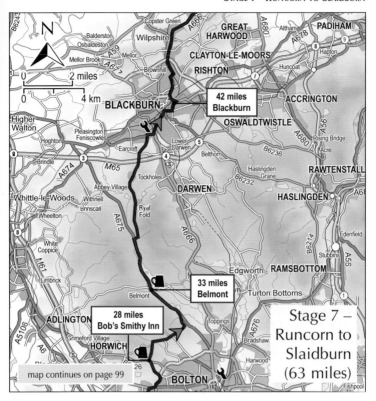

Lostock railway station (SD 674 086) and cycle straight on along Rumworth Road and Lostock Junction Lane to the junction with the A673 Chorley New Road (SD 674 093), on the outskirts of **Bolton**. At the junction of the A673 turn right and continue on for ¼ mile before turning left onto the A58 Victoria Road towards Bury. Remain on Victoria Road for approximately ½ mile and turn left into Old Kiln Lane, which is the B6402 (SD 681 101).

Stay on the B6402 for ¾ mile, to **Bob's Smithy Inn** (SD 675 110; 1448 Chorley Old Road, BL1 7PX; tel: 01204 84262), and go straight over the junction following the signs for Belmont (A675). From Bob's Smithy Inn cycle on for approximately 2¾ miles and turn left joining the A675 Belmont Road (SD 694 141). There will be views of Dingle Reservoir and Springs Reservoir to the right. Cycle along the A675 for 1¾ miles to the village of **Belmont** (SD 674 163), where the **Black Dog** (2–6 Church Street, Belmont BL7 8AB; tel: 01204 811218) is a convenient place for lunch. The pub is open daily 11.30am–11.00pm.

Leaving Belmont cycle out of the village for approximately 2 miles, passing Belmont Reservoir to the right and ascending to Old Man's Hill (SD 665 185) at 279m above sea level. Turn right into Crookfield Road, following the signs for Tockholes (SD 664 190). Cycle along this road for 1¾ miles into the village of Royal Fold, then continue for a further 1 mile into the village of Tockholes (SD 664 234). Remain on Tockholes Road for ¾ mile and cross over the M65 motorway (SD 665 243).

Having crossed the M65 on Tockholes Road, continue straight on for 1¼ miles to reach the junction with the A6062 Livesey Branch Road (SD 672 259). Turn right at this junction, which is a small roundabout; continue for a further ¼ mile and bear left into Albion Road, cycle along Albion Road for ¼ mile and turn right by the Empire Theatre building (SD 676 264) following the signs for Town Centre A666 and Clitheroe (A59).

Cycle along the A666 Bolton Road; after 110m there is an excellent and well-stocked cycle shop, **Ewood Bikes** (tel: 01254 55515; www.ewoodbikes.co.uk). The shop is a dedicated Shimano service centre and has a repair shop. Continue onwards from the cycle shop for approximately ¾ mile and at Town's Moor Junction turn left into Freckleton Street A6078, crossing over **Blackburn**'s iconic Wainwright Bridge (SD 682 274), named after Alfred Wainwright (1907–1991), the author of the seven-volume *Pictorial Guide to the Lakeland Fells* (www.wainwright.org.uk).

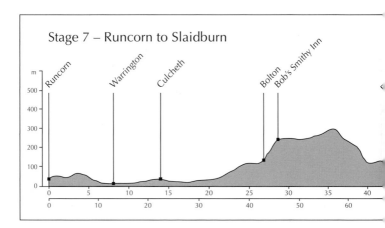

Stage 7 – Runcorn to Slaidburn

The Wainwright Bridge in Blackburn, named after one of Blackburn's most famous residents after a poll of local people

Having crossed Wainwright Bridge, cycle along Freckleton Street for 180m to the large junction at Canterbury Street. Follow the road as it bears left and then right round this unusually shaped junction before cycling along Byrom Street for approximately ¼ mile and turning right into King Street A674. Remain on King Street for a matter of 60m and turn left into Montague Street.

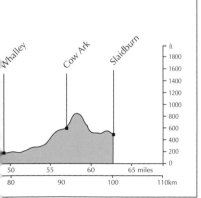

Cycle along Montague Street for ¼ mile and then bear right into Barbara Castle Way, following signs for Burnley A6078, Clitheroe, Whalley and Accrington. Cycle along Barbara Castle Way for ½ mile in the direction of the large and distinctive St Alban's Catholic Church (SD 686 284) and then turn left onto the A666 Larkhill, signed for Clitheroe and Whalley.

Cycle along the A666 for 4 miles to the village of Langho (SD 705 343). Once in the village cycle under

97

the metal rail bridge near Langho railway station and continue for a short distance before taking Whalley Road, the first road on the right (SD 708 348). This is a short-cut and avoids the large and busy roundabout at the junction of the A59. Cycle on for approximately ¼ mile and then bear right, remain on Whalley Road, cycling straight on towards Billington. Remain on this road for 1¼ mile and go under another railway bridge (SD 727 358) continuing to follow the signs for Whalley.

Cycle into the village of **Whalley** and along King Street, going over the bridge spanning the River Calder (SD 734 359), and continue straight on following signs for Mitton, Clitheroe and Calderstones Hospital. Continue through the village for approximately ½ mile and at a mini roundabout turn left into B6246 Station Road following signs for Mitton and the Three Fishes (SD 734 365). Cycle along the B6246 for approximately 2¼ miles from the village of Whalley; you will go under a railway bridge and then under the A59 (SD 726 366), and past Mitton Hall and the Aspinall Arms (SD 716 387) before crossing the River Ribble and then turning right into Church Lane. This turning is immediately after **Hillcrest Tearooms** (SD 715 390; tel: 01254 826573). Cycle along Church Lane for ½ mile, passing a handful of cottages, and at the give way sign (SD 713 396) go straight on. Continue for ½ mile and then bear left following signs for Bashall Eaves, Whitewell, Trough of Bowland (SD 709 404).

Cycle along this quiet lane for about a mile and at the staggered junction go straight over signed for Bashall Eaves. Continue for ¾ mile and at a fork in the road (SD 696 426) bear left signed for Browsholme Hall, Trough of Bowland, Whitewell and Dunsop Bridge.

Cycle on for ¼ mile before passing the **Red Pump Inn** public house (SD 696 432; www.theredpumpinn.co.uk; tel: 01254 826227) and then cycle on for a further ½ mile into the hamlet of **Bashall Eaves**. B&B accommodation can be found in this hamlet at Chapel Cottage B&B (www.chapelcottagebandb.co.uk; tel: 01254 826084).

Continue for a further 1¼ miles from Bashall Eaves and pass Browsholme Hall, built in 1507, which is the oldest surviving family home in the county of Lancashire and the ancestral home of the Parker family (www.browsholme.co.uk). Continue for a further ¾ mile into the tiny hamlet of **Cow Ark** (SD 672 454) and turn right at the telephone box following signs for Whitewell Direct Route. Cycle on for approximately ¼ mile and turn right following signs for Newton (SD 672 457).

You should now cycle along this peaceful country lane for 3½ miles to the junction (SD 702 498) at Hallgate Hill and turn left, following signs for Slaidburn. Continue on for another ½ mile, cycling down a very steep hill, before going over a bridge spanning the River Hodder and into the village of Newton in Bowland. Cycle past the **Parkers Arms**, Newton in Bowland (SD 696 504; www.parkersarms.co.uk; tel: 01200 446236) and ascend for the final 1½ miles towards the picturesque

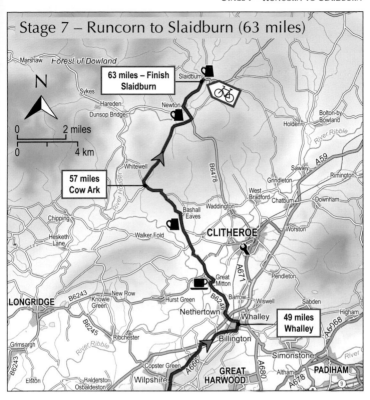

Stage 7 – Runcorn to Slaidburn (63 miles)

63 miles – Finish Slaidburn

57 miles Cow Ark

49 miles Whalley

village of **Slaidburn** via the B6478. A traditional Police House marks the ascent out of Newton in Bowland; the terrain then flattens and descends past Dunnow Hall.

On a warm and sunny evening there is an exceptional view across a lush meadow towards the River Hodder and Slaidburn. This timeless English landscape is part of the **Forest of Bowland**, a 312-square-mile AONB encompassing North Yorkshire and rural Lancashire. The Forest of Bowland is internationally important due to its heather moorland, blanket bog and rare birds. Besides being scientifically significant, the area is also visually stunning and thoroughly unspoilt, comprising dramatic moorland and wooded valleys, with dry-stone walls, picturesque farms and villages fringing the lowlands.

A damp day in the Forest of Bowland

Cycle into the village of Slaidburn and go past St Andrews Church, parts of which are around 560 years old. A short distance further on is King's House YHA (SD 712 524; BB7 3ER; tel: 01200 446656, email: slaidburn@yha.org.uk), a 30-bed hostel that occupies a former 17th-century coaching inn. Almost directly opposite Slaidburn YHA is the **Hark to Bounty** public house (www.harktobounty.co.uk; tel: 01200 446246; email manager@harktobounty.co.uk).

STAGE 8
Slaidburn to Keswick

Start	Hark to Bounty public house, Slaidburn (SD 712 524)
Finish	Keswick YHA (NY 267 235)
Distance	71 miles (114km)
Grade	Hard
Time	7½–8½ hours
Maps	OS Landranger 98: Wensleydale & Upper Wharfedale; OS Landranger 97: Kendal & Morecambe; OS Landranger 90: Penrith & Keswick
Refreshments	The Kings Arms, Main Street, **Burton-in-Kendal** (SD 530 765), tel: 01524 781409, meals and drinks. Pubs and cafés in Kendal, Staveley, Windermere, Ambleside and Grasmere.

The stage from Slaidburn in the Forest of Bowland to Keswick in the Lake District is one of the hardest yet most spectacular sections of the journey north. The first hours of the morning are notable for a long, tough climb through open expanses of grand moorland to the remains of the Cross of Greet at 427m above sea level, followed by a rapid descent to High Bentham before traversing country lanes to Kendal. Arriving in Kendal marks the start of the Lake District, where the fells, valleys and tarns have attracted visitors from as far back as the 18th century. Cycling north from this Lakeland town is always exciting because this is where the End to End can be won or lost. Over two days the route traverses the spectacular scenery of the Lake District National Park by way of the A591; the soaring fells that dominate the distant landscape will ensure even the most hardy long-distance cyclist will feel a little nervous. The A591 can be busy with both tourist and commuter traffic; on a wet, windy or scorching hot day, the road surface is unforgiving, sapping energy from the strongest legs.

The **Hark to Bounty** public house in the centre of **Slaidburn** is a lovely place to start the day's ride. Taking the road to the left of the nearby war memorial (SD 712 525), follow the sign for Bentham and Stocks Fishery. You will now be cycling along a narrow, hedge-lined country lane known as the Skaithe, which crosses Croasdale Brook.

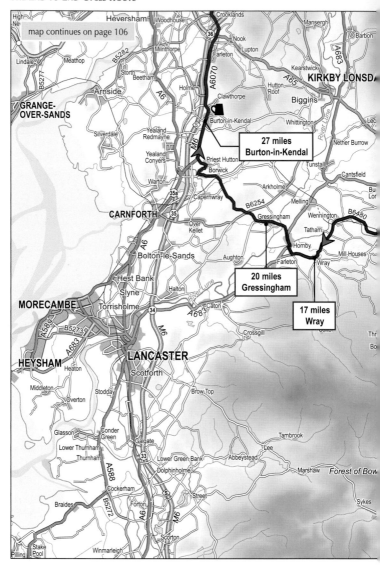

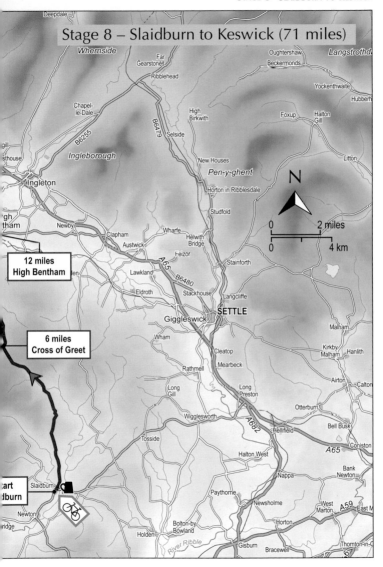

Stage 8 – Slaidburn to Keswick (71 miles)

The **Skaithe** is a tremendous road that ascends to the moorlands beyond Slaidburn. This route also provides an opportunity to observe a variety of species of birds; you may be fortunate and observe the hen harrier, the most important of the Bowland birds. The male is identifiable by its grey colour and black wing tips, while the female is brown with a white rump. Other sightings on the road between Slaidburn and High Bentham may include the short-eared owl, one of the few species of owl active in daylight, as well kestrels, merlins, ring ouzels, stonechats, curlews, peregrine falcons, buzzards and red grouse. The Skaithe ascends sharply from Slaidburn with views of Stocks Reservoir and Gisburn Forest away to the right; for those cyclists intending to return to the area, Gisburn Forest offers some of the best mountain biking in the north-west of England (**www.gisburnbiketrails.com**), with a range of purpose-built routes to suit all levels.

The Skaithe ascends for approximately 3 miles before finally beginning to descend just past Fellside Farm. After 4¾ miles from Slaidburn war memorial the road traverses the Cross of Greet Bridge (SD 703 590) at 251m above sea level.

Having crossed the bridge, ascend for approximately 2 miles to reach the remains of the Cross of Greet (SD 683 608), at 427m above sea level. This part of the route finds the single-track road clinging to the side of Lythe Fell while the River Hodder flows through the valley, which falls away to the left. In addition to the unfolding grandeur to the north there are spectacular, uninterrupted views for miles away to the south. The summit at the Cross of Greet is an exceptional place to take photographs of the morning's journey, before cycling onwards for

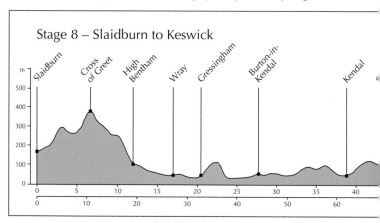

5¾ miles to the small town of High Bentham (SD 668 693). Having arrived in **High Bentham** turn left onto the B6480 Low Bentham Road following the sign for Lancaster.

Remain on the B6480, cycling for approximately 1½ miles into the village of Low Bentham (SD 650 694). Continue on this road for another 2¼ miles to the village of Wennington (SD 617 699), then for a further 1¾ miles to the village of **Wray** (SD 603 676). Cycle through Wray and after about a mile turn right following signs for Hornby and NCN90, the Lancashire Cycleway (SD 586 679).

Cycle on through the village of Hornby, crossing the bridge spanning the River Wenning (SD 585 684) and passing the post office on the right. Approximately ½ mile from Hornby Post Office turn left, signed for Gressingham and the Lancashire Cycleway NCN90 (SD 584 692). Continue along the road towards Gressingham, with the ruins of Castle Stede, a motte and bailey fortification, to the right. Cross over Loyn Bridge spanning the River Lune, continue for ¼ mile and turn right; you should now follow the road to the left and into the village of **Gressingham** (SD 571 699). Cycle through the village ascending for about a mile, following signs for Arkholme and Over Kellet; at the T junction with the B6254 (SD 559 706), turn left following signs for Over Kellet, Carnforth, Capernwray and Borwick.

Having turned left onto the B6254, cycle for a mere 100m before turning right into Borwick Road (SD 558 707). Continue for approximately 3 miles into the village of Borwick; at the telephone box (SD 526 731) in the village turn left following the sign for Carnforth. Cycle out of Borwick for approximately ¼ mile; at the next junction (SD 521 729) turn right into Kellet Lane signed for Burton-in-Kendal. Cycle onwards from this junction for approximately ½ mile, going over the

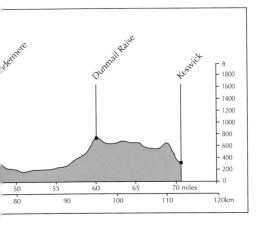

Lancaster Canal and passing Gatelands Caravan Park before turning right at the Longlands Hotel (SD 521 737) onto the A6070, signed for Burton-in-Kendal and Kendal. From Longlands Hotel cycle for approximately 2 miles on the A6070 into the village of **Burton-in-Kendal** (SD 530 765). The village is a convenient place for lunch; the **Kings Arms** public house (Main Street; tel: 01524 781409,

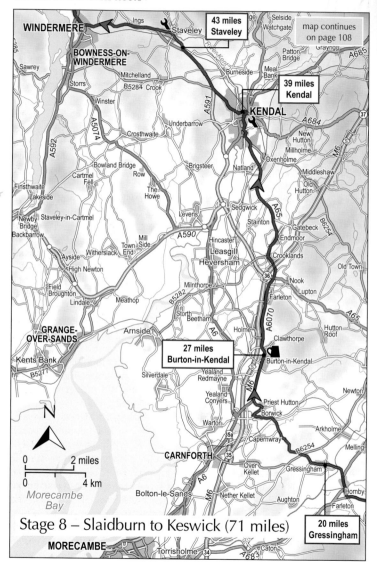

43 miles
Staveley

map continues
on page 108

39 miles
Kendal

27 miles
Burton-in-Kendal

20 miles
Gressingham

Stage 8 – Slaidburn to Keswick (71 miles)

Endmoor Millennium Clock

www.kingsarmsburton.co.uk; email kingsarmsburton@live.co.uk) offers both food and accommodation.

Leave Burton-in-Kendal and continue north for 4 miles to the roundabout (SD 536 824) at the junction of the A65 and A590; at this roundabout go straight ahead signed for Endmoor. Cycle on the A65 for 1¾ miles into Endmoor; look out for the distinctive Millennium Clock.

Remain on the A65, cycling for a further 3¾ miles from the Millenium Clock at Endmoor to Westmorland General Hospital, Kendal (SD 524 903). Continue past the hospital for approximately ¾ mile to the roundabout at the junction of the A65 and A6. Take the second exit off the roundabout (SD 518 916) onto Romney Road, following the sign for Windermere A591. Cycle along Romney Road for ¼ mile, going over Romney Road Bridge, which spans the River Kent; at the traffic lights turn right into Milnthorpe Road signed for the Town Centre.

Cycle on from the traffic lights for ¾ mile using Milnthorpe Road, Kirkland and Highgate into the centre of **Kendal**. At the junction of Highgate and Allhallows Lane go through a *No Entry* sign (bicycles **are** exempt) and continue to cycle along Highgate, passing the distinctive Kendal Town Hall (SD 515 926). Cycle onwards for ¼ mile, then bear left onto the A5284 Windermere Road ascending for a further 1½ miles to Strickland Ketel roundabout (SD 497 946) at the junction of the A591, A5284 and B5284.

At Strickland Ketel roundabout take the third exit signed A591 Windermere. **Take care** as this is a busy road; continue along the A591 for approximately 2 miles then turn right towards **Staveley**, following the NCN6 cycle route (SD 477 973). Cycle along Kendal Road for approximately ¾ mile into the village (SD 470 984). Staveley is home to one of the largest independent bicycle shops in the country: **Wheelbase** in the Mill Yard is a superb place to replenish any kit before the Lake District. Having gazed at their huge array of stock return to the main road through the village and bear left onto Windermere Road, cycling on for ½ mile before turning right and rejoining the A591 (SD 460 984), using the cycle path (NCN6) that runs on the footpath at the side of the A591. Remain on the NCN6 for approximately 1½ miles, at which point the cycle path crosses the carriageway

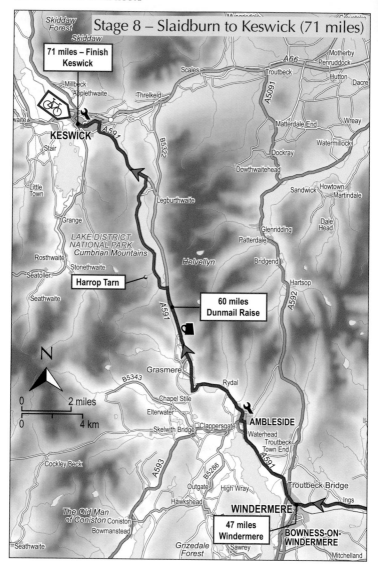

Stage 8 – Slaidburn to Keswick (71 miles)

71 miles – Finish
Keswick

60 miles
Dunmail Raise

Harrop Tarn

47 miles
Windermere

N

0   2 miles
0   4 km

to run alongside the left-hand side of the A591. After crossing the A591 cycle on for a further 1½ miles into **Windermere** and cycle through the town to St Mary's Church, Church Street (SD 410 988), which is an easily identifiable reference point on the left of the road. With the church on the left continue on the A591 for a further 1 mile passing through Troutbeck Bridge village (NY 404 003), where there is again the opportunity to use the cycle path NCN6, which runs at the side of the carriageway for certain parts of the route north to Ambleside.

Remain on the A591 from Troutbeck Bridge for approximately 3 miles to the small town of Ambleside (NY 376 045), then continue on the A591 following signs for Keswick. Cycle on for a further 4 miles to the charming village of **Grasmere** (NY 342 070).

This diminutive Lakeland village now houses the **Wordsworth Museum and Art Gallery** (LA22 9SH; **www.wordsworth.org.uk**; tel: 01539 463524), which is open throughout the year; adult admission currently costs £7.50. The museum incorporates Dove Cottage (NY 343 069), the former home of the great romantic poet William Wordsworth, who moved into the cottage with his younger sister Dorothy in the winter of 1799. Wordsworth wrote some of his greatest poetry while living in Grasmere, where he resided until 1808. Wordsworth and many of his family are buried in nearby St Oswalds Church (NY 338 073).

Dove Cottage in Grasmere, the charming former home of William Wordsworth and his family

Thirlmere – a classic Lakeland panorama

The final stage from Grasmere to Keswick is notable for a tough ascent from Grasmere, with exceptional views of a number of Lake District fells to the left and right. In terms of navigation; cycle out of Grasmere and remain on the A591 for 1¼ miles to the **Travellers Rest** public house (tel: 01539 435604), which marks the start of a 1½ mile ascent to the AA Box at **Dunmail Raise** (NY 327 117), at an altitude of 238m above sea level.

Cycle on from the AA Box for 1¼ miles towards Keswick, then turn left off the A591 (NY 325 129) following a blue cycle-route sign for Keswick via Castlerigg Stone Circle. The route round Thirlmere, with the towering presence of Helvellyn to the east, provides a rare treat for cyclists – a classic Lakeland panorama and the opportunity for a little fun with a swim in Harrop Tarn a short distance to the west of Thirlmere, one of the UK's most beautiful wild swimming locations.

To find **Harrop Tarn** (NY 312 137) follow the NCN6 as it skirts Thirlmere, look out for Dob Gill car park (NY 317 140), then take the footpath from the car park for approximately ¼ mile for a well-earned dip. The cycling charity Sustrans (**www.sustrans.org.uk/map**) have recently teamed up with the Outdoor Swimming Society **www.outdoorswimmingsociety.com**, adding hundreds of other outdoor swimming locations to the Sustrans online mapping facility.

From Dob Gill car park cycle on for 3¾ miles, pausing briefly at a distinctive plaque at the northern end of Thirlmere (NY 309 189).

THE BATTLE FOR THIRLMERE

This plaque commemorates the work of Manchester Corporation, proclaiming that the first stone was laid on 22 August 1890 towards the construction of an embankment on the lake. Behind the construction of the embankment lies a tale of Victorian environmental protest, with the water supply to Manchester to fuel the Industrial Revolution being at the heart of the issue.

The Manchester Corporation plaque at Thirlmere

In the 1840s the city fathers of Manchester had built reservoirs in the Peak District to supply the city. A generation later they were no longer sufficient to meet the growing demand for water. New reservoirs were needed and the spotlight fell on Thirlmere, the second highest lake in the Lake District. The plan was to dam the lake, raise the water level by 15m and then pipe water 100 miles to Manchester.

The Thirlmere Defence Association formed, a group vehemently opposed to the project, which argued that flooding the lake would ruin its character, impacting on the natural beauty of the Lake District as a whole. The association had wide-ranging support, from vociferous local land and property owners with distinctly parochial interests, keen to obtain the most favourable compensation, through to supporters from around the world who argued that the landscape of Wordsworth and Samuel Coleridge should be left unspoilt, as its beauty belonged to the nation.

The project was delayed by these protests but ultimately it went ahead, with the first water pumped to Manchester in 1894.

After following the NCN6 for 4¾ miles round Thirlmere, turn left, rejoining the A591 (NY 316 195) for the final push into **Keswick**. Having rejoined the A591 stay on this road for approximately 5 miles, going past Dale Bottom campsite (NY 294 219), before a short, steep descent into Keswick on the A591, Castlerigg Brow and Chestnut Hill. At the foot of Chestnut Hill follow the A5271 Penrith Road as it sweeps round to the left, with River Greta to the right, cycle on for ¾ mile before turning right into Station Street where you will find Keswick YHA on the left-hand side of the road, adjacent to the river (NY 267 235).

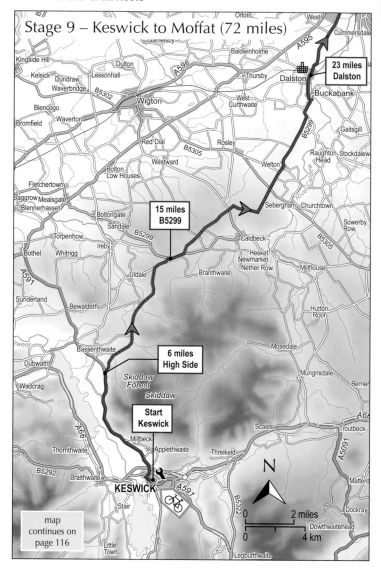

Stage 9 – Keswick to Moffat (72 miles)

23 miles
Dalston

15 miles
B5299

6 miles
High Side

**Start
Keswick**

KESWICK

map
continues on
page 116

N

0   2 miles
0   4 km

STAGE 9
Keswick to Moffat

Start	Keswick war memorial (NY 268 234)
Finish	Moffat town centre (NT 084 055)
Distance	72 miles (116km)
Grade	Hard
Time	7½–8½ hours
Maps	OS Landranger 85: Carlisle & Solway Firth; OS Landranger 78: Nithsdale & Annadale
Refreshments	**Dalston** (NY 369 504), snacks and drinks; Crumbs, 14 The Square, tel: 01228 711192, sandwiches and baguettes; Gretna Bakery and Café, 15 High Street, **Longtown** (NY 380 685), tel: 01228 792508, meals and drinks

This stage commences with a hard, uncompromising stretch of cycling along the flank of Skiddaw at Bassenthwaite Common before reaching higher ground at Faulds Brow, at which point the End to End route descends into Carlisle. In the city there is some urban cycling and then a short and challenging stretch on the A7 before turning off into quiet lanes to reach Longtown. From Longtown the route heads north crossing the border into Scotland, before a long flat section of the NCN74 cycle route through Lockerbie and onwards to Moffat.

The war memorial (NY 268 234) close to **Keswick** YHA is a convenient location from which to start and make an easy exit from the town. Turn right into Victoria Street A5271, identifiable by the pedestrian crossing; continue along this road for ¼ mile, following the road as it bears to the left before reaching the junction of Bank Street and Main Street. Turn right at this junction to continue on the A5271; the road crosses over the River Greta (NY 263 237) and at the Catholic Church of Our Lady of the Lakes (NY 261 239), with its distinctive copper roof, continue on Crosthwaite Road A5271, following the road as it bears round sharply to the right. Cycle along this road for ½ mile to the roundabout at the junction of the A66 (NY 264 244), go straight over at the roundabout taking the A591 signed for Carlisle.

From the roundabout, remain on the A591 for approximately 4¾ miles to **High Side**, enjoying the stunning views of the River Derwent and Bassenthwaite Lake away to the left and Skiddaw to the right. Having cycled to the hamlet of High Side (NY 235 306) turn right; the turning is identifiable by a bus stop and a Royal Mail postbox; follow the sign for Orthwaite. Cycle along this quiet country lane for ¾ mile to the next junction before following the sign for Uldale and Caldbeck. Continue on for a further ¼ mile, passing Peter House Farm on the left-hand side of the lane (NY 250 324). At the next significant junction (NY 253 330) cycle onwards following the signs for Orthwaite and Uldale. Continue from this junction for a further 1½ miles, and at the next crossroads (NY 258 351) cycle straight over following the sign for Caldbeck. Continue on from the crossroads for approximately 2 miles to the next junction and turn right following signs for Caldbeck (NY 268 378).

Remain on this country lane for another 1¼ miles before turning left (NY 287 385) following signs indicating Carlisle and Wigton. Cycle along this road for 2½ miles to the junction with the **B5299** (which is a tremendous location for savouring the stunning views towards Carlisle and the north), then continue straight over following the signs for Carlisle B5299 (NY 316 415).

Remain on the B5299 for 7½ miles into the village of **Dalston** (NY 369 504). This is a good place to stock up with snacks and drinks, and the friendly staff at **Crumbs** (14 The Square; tel: 01228 711192) will take advance orders for sandwiches and baguettes. Leave Dalston and continue to cycle on the B5299 for a further 3¾ miles into **Carlisle**, with Dixons chimney marking the entrance to city. Cycle along Shaddongate to the traffic lights at the junction of Bridge Street, with the former Globe public house directly ahead. Turn right at the traffic lights (NY 395 561) and use the cycle lane at the side of the A595 carriageway, continuing onwards for approximately ¼ mile to reach the imposing structure of Carlisle Castle.

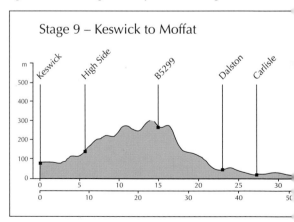

Stage 9 – Keswick to Moffat

The outer wall of Carlisle Castle

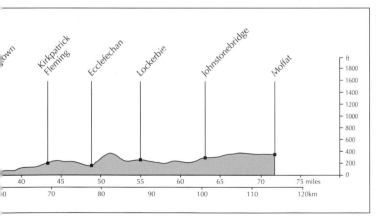

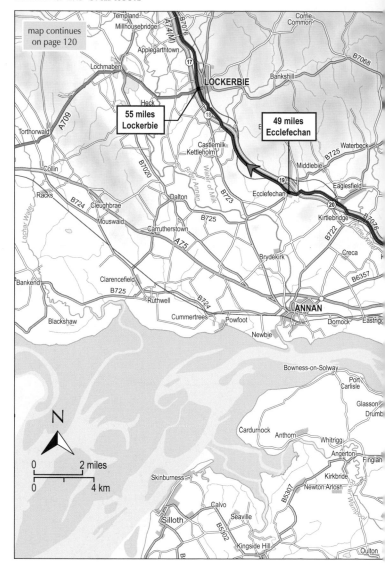

map continues
on page 120

55 miles
Lockerbie

49 miles
Ecclefechan

N

0   2 miles
0   4 km

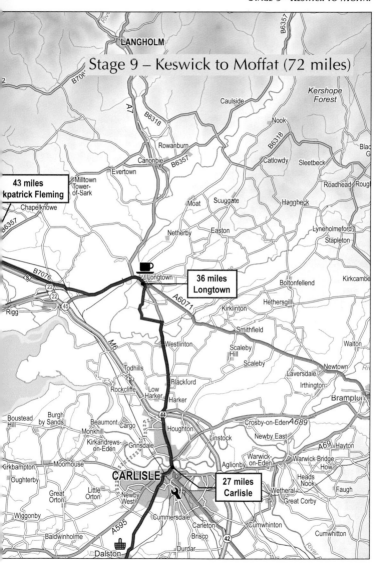

Stage 9 – Keswick to Moffat (72 miles)

LANGHOLM

Kershope Forest

Caulside

Nook

Rowanburn

Canonbie

Evertown

Catlowdy

Sleetbeck

Roadhead

43 miles
Kirkpatrick Fleming

Milltown
Tower-
of-Sark

Chapelknowe

Moat

Scuggate

Haggbeck

Lyneholmeford

Stapleton

Netherby

Easton

Longtown

36 miles
Longtown

Boltonfellend

Kirkcambe

Rigg

Kirklinton

Hethersgill

Smithfield

Westlinton

Scaleby
Hill

Scaleby

Walton

Todhills

Blackford

Laversdale

Newtown

Rockcliffe

Low
Harker

Harker

Irthington

Brampton

Boustead
Hill

Burgh
by Sands

Beaumont

Cargo

Crosby-on-Eden

Monkhill

Houghton

Newby East

Kirkandrews-
on-Eden

Grinsdale

Linstock

Warwick-
on-Eden

Aglionby

Warwick-Bridge

How

Kirkbampton

Moorhouse

Heads
Nook

Faugh

Oughterby

Great
Orton

Little
Orton

Newby
West

CARLISLE

27 miles
Carlisle

Wetheral

Great Corby

Wiggonby

Cummersdale

Carleton

Brisco

Cumwhinton

Cumwhitton

Baldwinholme

Durdar

Dalston

117

In AD72 the Romans settled in Carlisle and built a large fort from earth and wood, part of which is now beneath **Carlisle Castle**. The Romans named the thriving settlement that existed to serve the fort *Luguvalium*. The Roman fort served a number of key functions: as an administrative centre, a supply base for other garrisons on Hadrian's Wall and an important stopping-off point for Roman troops heading north to invade Scotland. After the Roman occupation of Carlisle ended in the fourth century, it is thought that the location was occupied by native Britons for at least a century. In 685 it was part of the Northumbrian royal estate, before being overrun by Viking invaders at the end of the ninth century. By 1092 King William Rufus had gained control of the castle and he built a substantial wooden fortification, which was replaced by King Henry I with stone in the early part of the 12th century. Today the main part of the castle that can be seen from the roadway is the impressive Outer Gatehouse, built around 1160 and altered in 1378. Over the years this structure has served a number of purposes, including exchequer offices for the sheriff of Cumberland, a small barrack block for soldiers and even a sergeants' mess (**www.english-heritage.org.uk**).

Cycle past the castle for ¼ mile to reach Hardwicke Circus Roundabout (NY 402 564), and take the A7 north for approximately 2¼ miles to Junction 44 of the M6 (NY 395 599). At this large, busy junction take the second exit signed for A7(N) Hawick and Galashiels, and continue on the A7 for approximately 2¾ miles into the hamlet of Westlinton (NY 393 646). **Take care** on the A7 as this is a busy road used by numerous heavy goods vehicles. In the hamlet of Westlinton turn left, following signs for Rockcliffe. This left turn is also marked by a telephone box and an NCN7 sign. Some riders may wish to stay on the A7, which goes directly into Longtown. However, the quiet route is strongly recommended. From the Westlinton turning cycle towards Rockcliffe for ¼ mile and turn right onto the NCN7 (NY 388 645). A Sustrans marker leads the way. Cycle along the NCN7, which is a disused railway line with a good gravel and shale surface, for about a mile before emerging onto a quiet lane and turning left in front of a large green-coloured barn (NY 383 661). Cycle along this quiet lane for approximately 1¾ miles to the junction with the Carlisle Road in Longtown.

Turn left onto the A7 Carlisle Road, cycle onwards for approximately ½ mile, going through the centre of **Longtown** (NY 380 685) where **Gretna Bakery and Café** (15 High Street, CA6 5UA; tel: 01228 792508) is a convenient place for lunch in inclement weather. Continue through the town for approximately ½ mile, crossing Longtown Bridge over the River Esk (NY 378 689) before turning left onto the A6071, signed for Gretna. Cycle on the A6071 for approximately 2 miles; turn right signed for Gretna Green (NY 346 678). Remain on this road for about a mile,

Not an original photo stop, but an unavoidable one!

crossing the River Sark, which marks a significant landmark on the End to End: the border between England and Scotland.

After stopping for photographs on the border, cycle onwards, going under an iron bridge to a roundabout (NY 329 681). Take the second exit, signed for Springfield, into Main Street. Cycle onwards for approximately ½ mile to a T junction at the junction with the B7076, and turn right following signs for Gretna and Gretna Green (NY 324 683). Remain on the B7076 for approximately 3 miles into the village of **Kirkpatrick Fleming** (NY 278 705) before cycling onwards for approximately 6¼ miles to **Ecclefechan** (NY 193 745).

There is an excellent museum at the **Arched House** in the High Street celebrating Ecclefechan as the birthplace of one of the central figures of Victorian Britain: Thomas Carlyle (1795–1881), the writer, philosopher and historian. Carlyle spent his early years in the village before going up to Edinburgh University. He was a gifted scholar, going on to become an acclaimed writer, famous for works such as *Sartor Resartus*, *The French Revolution* and his epic six-volume *History of Friedrich II of Prussia*. His former home is now maintained by the National Trust for Scotland, and it holds a significant collection of Carlyle memorabilia. Furnished in an authentic style, it gives a snapshot of life

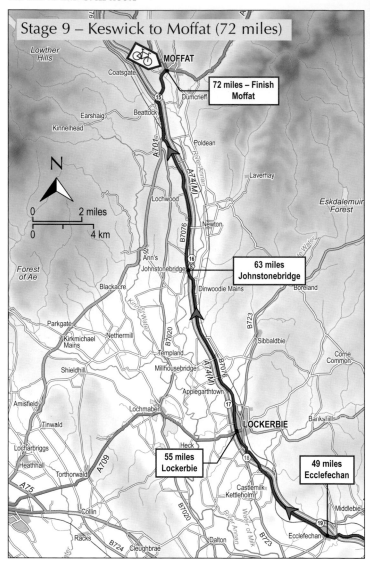

Stage 9 – Keswick to Moffat (72 miles)

72 miles – Finish Moffat

63 miles Johnstonebridge

55 miles Lockerbie

49 miles Ecclefechan

Statue of Thomas Carlyle in Ecclefechan

in a Victorian household. The museum is open Monday to Friday 1.30pm–5.00pm, from 1 June to 30 September. Admission is currently £3 for adults (**www.nts.org.uk**).

From the Arched House rejoin the End to End route by cycling along the High Street into Burnbank Street, where you will see a statue of the great man himself (NY 190 748): this is a bronze replica of Sir Joseph Edgar Boehm's statue of Carlyle, which stands in Chelsea Embankment Gardens, London.

From the statue continue for ¼ mile to rejoin the B7076 (NY 190 748), continuing north for approximately 6 miles on the NCN74 to the town of Lockerbie (NY 133 815). The NCN74 cycle route bypasses **Lockerbie** to the west, following the B7076 and the A74(M) northwards. Remain on the NCN74 for approximately 7¼ miles to the village of **Johnstonebridge** (NY 101 921), then from Johnstonebridge continue on the NCN74 for a further 7¼ miles to Junction 15 of the A74(M) (NT 078 029). At the roundabout turn right following the signs for **Moffat**, and cycle on the A701 for approximately 1¾ miles into the town centre (NT 084 055). One legacy of Moffat's popularity as a Victorian spa town is the numerous establishments of all sizes offering accommodation for the passing traveller. End to Enders should have no trouble finding a comfortable place to stay.

STAGE 10
Moffat to Loch Lomond

Start	Moffat town centre (NT 084 055)
Finish	Loch Lomond SYHA (NS 368 834) or Balloch town centre (NS 390 818)
Distance	85 miles (137km) or 83 miles (134km)
Grade	Hard
Time	8–9 hours
Maps	OS Landranger 71: Lanark & Upper Nithsdale; OS Landranger 64: Glasgow; OS Landranger 63: Firth of Clyde; OS Landranger 56: Loch Lomond & Inveraray
Refreshments	Happendon Services (Cairn Lodge) (NS 851 338); Co-operative store, Union Street, **Larkhall** (NS 762 513), snacks and drinks

The End to End stage from Moffat to Loch Lomond SYHA, although lengthy, is a relatively straightforward affair and navigation should not prove to be particularly difficult. There is a choice of two routes for departing from Moffat. The main route is hilly and spectacular, but there is an alternative along flatter terrain if you prefer. The first three hours' cycling involve a steady ascent from Moffat towards Glasgow, which can be strenuous, particularly in bad weather. On the outskirts of Glasgow the terrain flattens, but this part of the route can be busy with urban business and commuter traffic heading into the city. There is one key navigational waypoint at Cambuslang that requires a certain amount of concentration; it leads to the NCN7 and a memorable traffic-free ride along the riverscape of one of Europe's most vibrant cities. A larger scale map is provided to help you navigate this section.

Alternative start from Moffat to Junction 14 of the A74(M)

For a relatively flat start to this stage of the End to End, retrace the final part of yesterday's stage for 1¾ miles, back along the A701 to Junction 15 of the A74(M) (NT 078 029). At this roundabout take the third exit signed for Abington B7076 and use the NCN74 cycle route. Continue north on the NCN74 for approximately 13½ miles to Junction 14 of the A74(M) (NS 958 186).

To leave Moffat by the hillier, more scenic route, head north on the A701 Edinburgh Road (NT 084 056) for 2½ miles to reach the B719, Greenhillstairs. Turn left at this junction (NT 065 085), cycle onwards for approximately 2¾ miles, then turn right (NT 035 112) to join the B7076 before cycling north for 7¾ miles to Junction 14 of the A74(M) (NS 958 186).

With the alternative start route converging with the main at Junction 14 of the A74(M), continue to cycle along the NCN74 for approximately 4½ miles into the village of **Abington** (NS 932 234), and go through the village for ¾ mile to the roundabout at Junction 13 of A74(M). Here, take the second exit signed for Douglas (B7078) (NS 928 246) and continue to follow the NCN74 north.

Remain on the NCN74 (B7078) for approximately 8 miles to its junction with the A70. At this T junction (NS 856 326) turn right onto the A70 following signs for Coalburn and Lanark; the junction is also marked by a Sustrans National Cycle Network sign.

Having turned right at this T junction cycle on for approximately ¼ mile, going under the M74 motorway; at the roundabout turn left signed for Glasgow B7078, Coalburn and Services. Continue onwards, cycling past **Happendon Services** (Cairn Lodge) (NS 851 338) for approximately 1½ miles to the next roundabout (NS 848 348) where you should follow the signs for NCN74, Glasgow B7078, Coalburn and Lesmahagow. Cycle back under the M74 motorway for 160m to another roundabout, and at this roundabout take the second significant exit onto the NCN74 and B7078. Cycle on for a further 160m and fork left onto the B7078, the NCN74, towards Glasgow (NS 845 350).

Remain on the B7078 for approximately 4½ miles, passing through Lesmahagow (NS 819 394) to the roundabout at Junction 10 of the M74 (NS 812 414). Negotiate the roundabout and take the second exit, which is signed Glasgow B7078 (A72). Remain on the B7078 for a further 2 miles into **Blackwood** (NS 795 432) and continue on the B7078 Carlisle Road for approximately 5½ miles into the town of **Larkhall** (NS 762 513). The **Co-op** in Union Street is a convenient place to stock up with snacks and drinks. Cycle out of Larkhall on the B7078 Carlisle Road for approximately 1¼ miles – the B7078 merges with the A72 (NS 751 531) – then continue onwards from this junction for about a mile to the entrance to **Chatelherault Country Park** (NS 742 543); a tranquil setting in which to enjoy a well-earned break and a sandwich.

The grounds of **Chatelherault Country Park** cover nearly 500 acres and were once part of Hamilton Palace, one of the grandest country houses in Scotland, formerly owned by the Duke of Hamilton. The palace itself was demolished in 1921 and the centrepiece of the park now comprises the former hunting lodge and summerhouse, built in 1732 to the designs of William Adam. At

map continues on page 126

Stockbriggs

Coalburn
Bellfield
Braehead

Rigside

11

Uddington

12

30 miles
Happendon Service

New

Glenbuck
Parish
Holm

Glespin
Hazelside

Douglas

Carmacoup

Duglas Water

M74

B7078

Rober

rk

Kames

A7

Crawfordjohn

Duneaton Water

B740

Abington

S

13

E

A74(M

Fingland

Corsebank

B7040

E

Kirkland

Lagrae

Carco

Leadhills

B7197

Kirkconnel

Knockenstob
Crawick

Wanlockhead

G

SANQUHAR

Ulzieside

Auchengruith

River Nith

Mennock

Lowther
Hills

skeoch

Enterkinfoot

Durisdeermill

High
Enoch

Stage 10 – Moffat to Loch Lomond (85 miles)

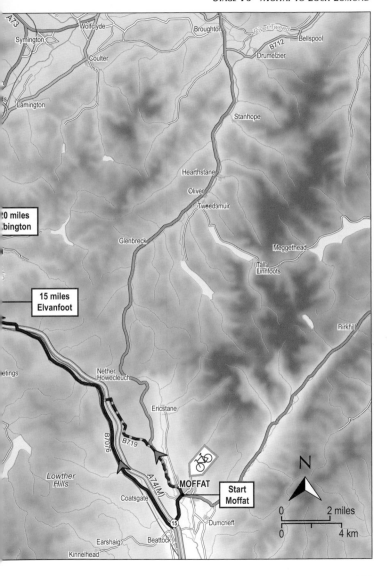

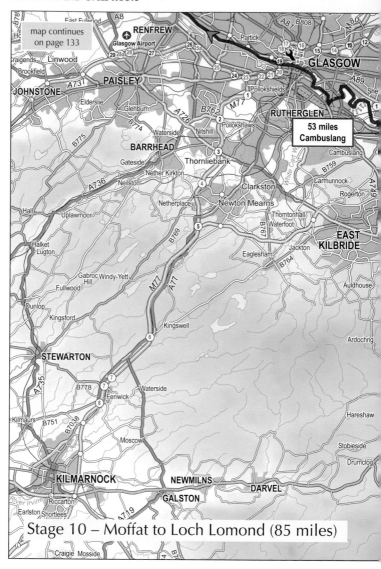

map continues
on page 133

53 miles
Cambuslang

Stage 10 – Moffat to Loch Lomond (85 miles)

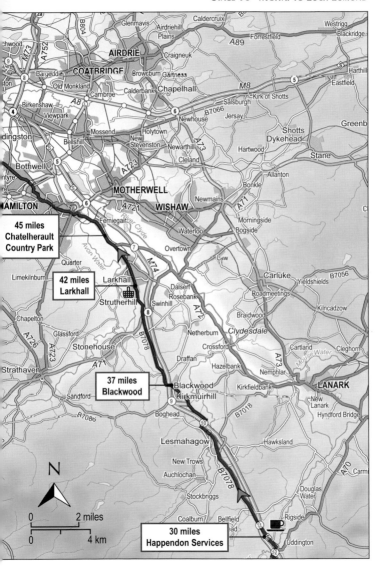

one time the hunting lodge also seemed destined for demolition after it fell into serious disrepair, and its survival was by no means assured. However, after a prolonged period of renovation between 1979 and 1987 the lodge is now fully restored. The visitor centre is open to the public Monday to Saturday 10.00am–5.00pm, and Sunday 12.00pm–5.00pm, while the main house is open Monday to Thursday 10.00am–4.00pm (**www.visitlanarkshire. com**; tel: 01698 426213).

From the calm surroundings of Chatelherault Country Park, continue along the A72 for a further 1¼ miles to the junction of the A72 Townhead Street and A723 Duke Street in Hamilton (NS 727 553). Turn left at the traffic lights, following the signs for Strathaven, Rutherglen and East Kilbride A723. Cycle on for approximately 180m to the junction of Duke Street and High Patrick Street. Move to the centre lane; follow signs for the A724 Rutherglen and East Kilbride and cycle straight ahead, passing Marks and Spencer in Duke Street to the immediate right.

Continue onwards for approximately 275m, with the road ascending gently; remain in the centre lane and go straight over at the junction into Brandon Street: the correct direction of travel is signified by having SPT Travel Centre on your right and Hamilton Rail (NS 722 553) on the left. Continue onwards from Hamilton Rail along the A724 Brandon Street, cycling on the A724 for a further 6¼ miles before turning right at a very important navigational waypoint marked by **Cambuslang** parish church (NS 645 605) at the junction of the A724 Hamilton Road and Clydeford Road. The waypoint is also signposted A763 Carlisle, Stirling and Edinburgh. The distinctive church was constructed between 1961 and 1966.

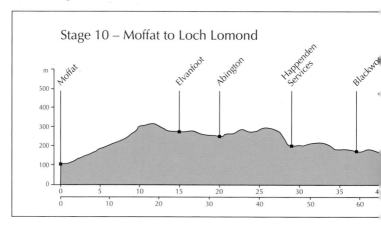

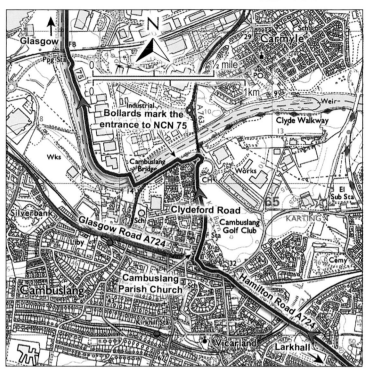

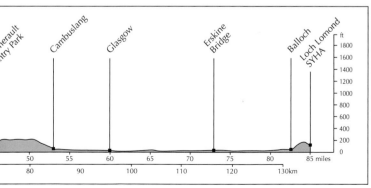

Formerly known as St Andrews, it is easily identifiable by its shallow pitched roof and 1960s-style architecture.

Having turned right into Clydeford Road, continue on for a ½ mile and at the next roundabout take the first exit (left) onto the A763 Bridge Street. After 20m four bollards and a lampost on the right of the road mark the entrance to the NCN75 (NS 645 613).

Cycle through the bollards marked by a sign for the NCN75 and the Clyde Walkway and turn left signed for Dalmarnock, Bridgeton and Glasgow. This marks the start of a very enjoyable stretch of the End to End as the route follows the north bank of the River Clyde through the very heart of **Glasgow**, an area rich in industrial history and now one of the most exciting riverscapes in Europe.

GLASGOW

Facing geographically westward towards the Americas placed Glasgow in a strong position to take advantage of early transatlantic trade in tobacco, and later cotton. By 1760 Glasgow was the premier tobacco port in Britain, importing around 33 million pounds in weight per year, which was then re-exported all over Europe. The trade brought serious wealth into the hands of the city's tobacco lords. In the early years, all the imported tobacco leaf was landed at Greenock or Port Glasgow, but onward distribution was impeded by the shallowness of the River Clyde. The wealthy tobacco lords lobbied for the river to be deepened to allow bigger ships to access the city, and the finest engineering talent of the day, such as James Smeaton and Thomas Telford, developed innovative ways of deepening the river, further opening up the city to trade.

The American War of Independence interrupted the Glasgow tobacco trade and it never recovered its previous importance; however, the void was quickly filled by cotton, bringing about the textile phase of Glasgow's Industrial Revolution. Business on the Clyde was booming, which in turn demanded more dredging and widening of the river. By 1818 industrial vessels could navigate the Clyde as far as Broomielaw (near the Kingston Bridge, NS 580 649). Crucially, the textile industry brought with it developments in power-driven machinery, science and technology, with water-powered cotton mills a common feature of Glasgow. The first Bolton and Watt steam engines began to appear in the textile mills in the 1780s; these technological innovations laid the foundations for the heavy industry that would later dominate the banks of the Clyde. After 1840 the textile phase of industrialisation stalled, with supplies of cotton interrupted by the American

Civil War. By the end of the 19th century, shipbuilding and metalworking had overtaken cotton to become the most important industry on the Clyde.

It was through shipbuilding that Glasgow became famous throughout the world. Its zenith was reached in 1913 with the Clyde boasting 39 shipyards, which in a single year launched almost a fifth of the world's shipping tonnage. For the following six decades the Clyde shipbuilding industry enjoyed decidedly mixed fortunes: full order books to supply the navy in the First World War; lay offs and closures in the Great Depression; new naval orders in the Second World War; then a period of under-investment and foreign competition in the 1950s leading to industrial unrest and yard closures in the 1960s and 1970s. In recent years the Glasgow waterfront has undergone a significant urban renewal; with architecturally impressive buildings adding vitality and a distinct sense of regeneration and exuberance to the banks of the Clyde.

St Andrew's suspension bridge near Glasgow Green

To reach the very heart of Glasgow, cycle along the NCN75 for approximately 6½ miles from Clydeford Road, Cambuslang, to reach St Andrew's suspension bridge (NS 600 640). This is a 67m wrought-iron bridge, engineered by Neil Robson of Glasgow and built in 1854–55 to replace the ferry that transported workers across the River Clyde from Bridgeton and Calton to Hutchesontown. Cycle on from the suspension bridge onto Glasgow Green (NS 599 642).

> **Glasgow Green** is one of the oldest public parks in Scotland. Here you will find the impressive 44m-tall Nelson Monument (NS 597 644), financed by public donations and built in 1806 by the architect David Hamilton. This was the first monument in Britain to commemorate Lord Horatio Nelson's victories at Aboukir in 1798, Copenhagen in 1801 and Trafalgar in 1805. Other highlights on Glasgow Green are the resplendent Doulton Fountain (NS 603 641), the largest and best example of a terracotta fountain in the world, and the imposing gateway to Glasgow Green formed by the McLennan Arch (NS 595 645), designed by Robert and James Adam.

Cycle onwards from Glasgow Green for a further 1½ miles to the Clyde Auditorium, following signs for the NCN75 Bells Bridge, Paisley and Loch Lomond, then following signs for the NCN7.

> The **Clyde Auditorium** (NS 569 654) is an iconic landmark and part of the Scottish Exhibition and Conference Centre (SECC) complex, affectionately known as the Armadillo, which was designed and built to a strict budget by award-winning architects Foster and Partners between 1995 and 1997 for £27 million. It is one of a handful of European venues capable of hosting 3000 delegates, and boasts state of the art acoustics. Built from precast and bonded block concrete, steel and glass, the most striking feature of the construction is the roof, constructed by flopping huge rolls of aluminium over steel trusses to give the appearance of interlocking ships' hulls, a clear acknowledgement of Glasgow's shipbuilding tradition.

Leaving the Clyde Auditorium away to the right, cycle along the NCN7 as it forks left, back towards the River Clyde. Within 100m stands Bells Bridge (NS 568 653), the unique design of which involves a movable section that pivots to allow large vessels to pass through. The symmetrically curved bridge was built in 1988 to link the SECC with the Glasgow Garden Centre and is easily identified by the tapered pylon and the cables that radiate from its centre pier.

From Bells Bridge cycle onwards for ½ mile, following the NCN7 signed for Clydebank, Dumbarton and Loch Lomond. Remain on the NCN7, using the

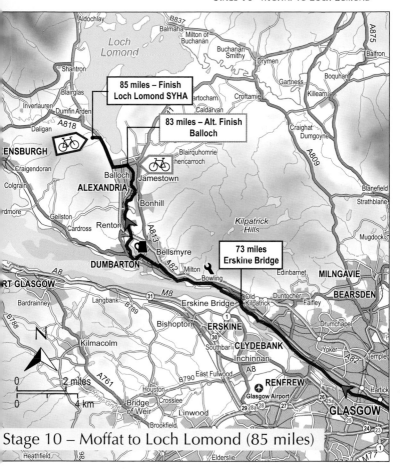

Stage 10 – Moffat to Loch Lomond (85 miles)

footbridge (NS 564 658) to cross over the A814 Pointhouse Road dual carriageway. There are excellent views of the three-masted museum ship SV Glenlee, built and rigged in 1896.

The **Glenlee** is known as the Tall Ship at Glasgow Harbour and is one of only five Clyde-built sailing vessels still afloat. It is also one of Glasgow's most popular visitor attractions (**www.thesquarerigger.com/glenlee**).

Close to the Glenlee is the Riverside Museum at Pointhouse Quay (NS 558 660; **www.glasgowlife.org.uk/museums**), which opened in June 2011. It was designed by award winning architects Zaha Hadid, and built at a cost of £74 million. The museum explores Glasgow's maritime and transport heritage and is expected to attract hundreds of thousands of visitors each year.

Descend from the A814 footbridge and follow NCN7 signs for Clydebank, Dumbarton and Loch Lomond. At the base of the footbridge is a Sustrans sign indicating 215 miles to Inverness and 19 miles to Loch Lomond. Cycle on the NCN7 for a further 5½ miles, following signs for Loch Lomond, to reach the Forth and Clyde Canal (NS 501 703).

Look out for the sculpture Bankies Bike, designed by artist John Crosby and unveiled by Mark Beaumont, the record-breaking round-the-world cyclist, in the summer of 2008. The sculpture is designed to help promote safe cycling in Clydebank. At Bankies Bike turn left, continuing to follow signs towards Loch Lomond. The End to End route now follows the tow path alongside the Forth and

Bankies Bike, in Clydebank, by John Crosby

Clyde Canal as far as Bowling and is also signed NCN7, Clydebank town centre, Dalmuir, Mountblow, Old Kilpatrick and Bowling.

> The **Forth and Clyde Canal** (38¾ miles long) is a visual remnant of Glasgow's early industrial growth. It was designed by John Smeaton and built between 1768 and 1790 as a man-made trade route, capable of carrying small, ocean-going vessels between the Firth of Clyde to the west and the Firth of Forth to the east. With its constant depth of 2.1m it was, towards the end of the 18th century, the preferred option for transporting cargo into the centre of Glasgow, but eventually it fell victim to competition from rail and road. The canal struggled on, remaining open for many more decades before it finally closed in 1963. It then lay derelict and disused for several years, but thanks to recent investment from the Millennium Link the canal is once again open, now for purely recreational pursuits.

Cycle alongside the canal on the NCN7 for approximately 3 miles to the Erskine Bridge (NS 465 726). There has been a ferry operating on the River Clyde in this area for centuries, but with the growth of traffic in Glasgow and an increasing need for quicker, more convenient means of transport and communication, work commenced on the Erskine Bridge in 1967. It took four years to build, at a cost of £10.5m, and was opened by HRH Princess Anne in July 1971. Go under the Erskine Bridge and continue for a further 1½ miles in the direction of Dumbarton, remaining on the NCN7 to Bowling Harbour, where you will find a bicycle work-shop at **Magic Cycles** (NS 451 735; tel: 01389 873433; www.magiccycles.co.uk). This is a handy place to stop for minor repairs before pushing on to Balloch and Loch Lomond.

Cycle on from Bowling Harbour following the NCN7 for a further 3½ miles into central **Dumbarton**. Navigation on the outskirts of the town is a little tricky as the NCN7 weaves through a housing estate, where you should take particular care not to miss the sign for the NCN7 at the junction of Third Avenue and Geils Avenue (NS 415 747). Once you are in central Dumbarton, the NCN7 cycle route is reasonably well signposted, although again you need to look out carefully for the NCN7 sign when going through the archway near Dumbarton Central railway station. Further vigilance is also required where the NCN7 passes **McCaff's Bar at the Railway Tavern**, 127 College Street (NS 397 755). It then progresses towards Loch Lomond via a cycle and pedestrian underpass, which can be seen from outside McCaff's.

Cycle through the underpass, continuing to follow the signs for NCN7 Loch Lomond. The key to navigation through Dumbarton is to cross the River Leven via Bridge Street (NS 393 754) and then turn immediately right to remain on the

Loch Lomond SYHA

NCN7 cycle path, which follows the course of the River Leven for the next 4½ miles towards Balloch and Loch Lomond.

Balloch finish

Finishing in **Balloch** (NS 390 818), after this lovely stretch of cycle path, is a pleasant alternative to carrying straight on to the youth hostel. The town offers a host of B&B and hotel accommodation, suitable for all budgets. With the marina acting as a reference point emerge from the cycle path onto Balloch Road, where you will find the Tourist Information Centre (tel: 01389 753533).

For those End to Enders staying at the SYHA Loch Lomond cycle onwards, with Balloch Tourist Information Centre on the right, for approximately ½ mile to a roundabout forming the junction of Balloch Road and Old Luss Road. At this roundabout turn left and continue for approximately 100m (you will pass McDonald's) and then negotiate the roundabout at the junction of the B867 with the A811 (NS 368 816). Turn right at this roundabout following signs for Glasgow and Crianlarich. You should then cycle up the hill, remaining on the A811 for ½ mile to reach Stoneymollan roundabout (NS 381 815); take the A82, second exit, signed for Crianlarich, Tarbet, Helensburgh and Luss. Cycle along the A82 and after 1¼ miles turn left for **Loch Lomond Youth Hostel** (NS 368 834; Auchendennan, Arden, G83 8RA; tel: 01389 850226).

136

STAGE 11
Loch Lomond to Glencoe

Start	Loch Lomond SYHA (NS 368 834)
Finish	Glencoe SYHA (NN 118 576) or Glencoe Village (NN 102 588)
Distance	68 miles (109km) or 71 miles (114km)
Grade	Moderate/Hard
Time	6½–7½ hours
Maps	OS Landranger 50: Glen Orchy & Loch Etive; OS Landranger 41: Ben Nevis
Refreshments	**Tyndrum**: the Real Food Café, tel: 01838 400235 (fish and chips) or the Green Welly, tel: 01838 400271

This stage of the End to End offers some of the most magnificent scenery of the entire journey. However, certain stretches of the A82 between Balloch and Glencoe can be very busy, especially in the summer months. Tourist coaches, HGVs, high-powered motorcycles and ordinary commuter traffic all use this route to travel north towards Glencoe, Fort William and the Far North. End to Enders are strongly advised to wear high-visibility vests and ensure that their bicycle lights are working correctly. Carry warm weather clothing too, as the weather in the Pass of Glencoe can deteriorate quickly, even in summer.

To begin the day's stage leave **Loch Lomond Youth Hostel** (NS 368 834), cycle down the lane to the junction with the A82 (NS 373 834) and turn left. Continue on the A82 for 1¼ miles to Arden roundabout (NS 359 846) and then use the West Loch Lomond Cycle Path NCN40, which runs alongside the shore of the loch. Remain on the West Loch Lomond Cycle Path for approximately 13½ miles into the hamlet of Tarbet, turn right in Tarbet (NN 319 045) and follow signs for Crianlarich and Fort William on the A82.

Cycle out of Tarbet and stay on the A82 for approximately 8¼ miles, to the hamlet of **Ardlui** (NN 317 155). Continue through the hamlet and cycle for a further 8¼ miles to the village of Crianlarich (NN 384 251). Upon entering **Crianlarich** turn left, remaining on the A82 signed for Fort William, passing the Crianlarich Hotel (www.crianlarich-hotel.co.uk; tel: 01838 300272), which is situated on the

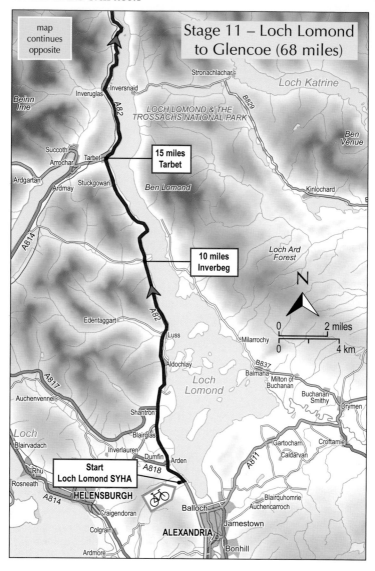

Stage 11 – Loch Lomond to Glencoe (68 miles)

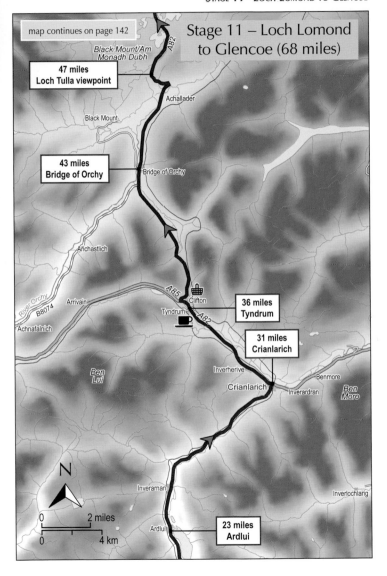

map continues on page 142

Black Mount/Am Monadh Dubh

Stage 11 – Loch Lomond to Glencoe (68 miles)

A82

47 miles
Loch Tulla viewpoint

Achallader

Black Mount

43 miles
Bridge of Orchy

Bridge of Orchy

Arichastlich

River Orchy

A85

Clifton

B8074

Arrivain

Tyndrum

A82

36 miles
Tyndrum

Achnafalnich

31 miles
Crianlarich

Ben
Lui

Inverherive

Crianlarich

Benmore

Ben
Moro

Inverardran

Inveraran

Inverlochlarig

N

0   2 miles
0   4 km

Ardlui

23 miles
Ardlui

139

Approching Glencoe

left-hand side of the road as you leave the village. Continue from Crianlarich for 4¾ miles to the village of **Tyndrum (NN 330 304)**, which is a perfect place to stop for lunch. Tyndrum boasts two excellent places to have a meal or to stock up with snacks: the Real Food Café and the Green Welly. **The Real Food Café** (www. therealfoodcafe.com; tel: 01838 400235) serves tasty fish and chips. **The Green Welly** is a renowned and popular choice with motorcyclists among others (www. thegreenwellystop.co.uk; tel: 01838 400271).

Continue on the A82 from Tyndrum for ½ mile to the junction of the A82 and A85 (NN 325 306) and turn right, following signs for the A82 to Fort William. Remain on the A82 for approximately 6½ miles to the **Bridge of Orchy** Hotel (NN 298 396; www. bridgeoforchy.co.uk) and continue onwards.

You will now be cycling through a spectacular part

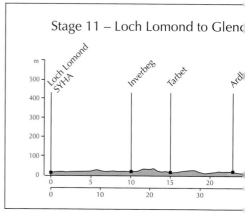

Stage 11 – Loch Lomond to Glenc

Buachaille Etive Mor on the way into Glencoe

of Scotland, with breathtaking views of Loch Tulla to the left. After a further 4½ miles from the Bridge of Orchy a lay-by and **viewpoint** (NN 308 452) make a superb place to enjoy the stunning Highland views, with a piper adding to the atmosphere at the weekend.

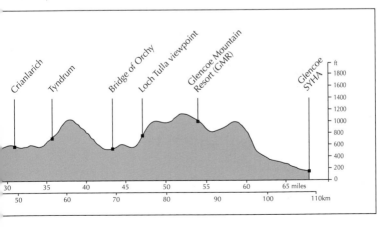

141

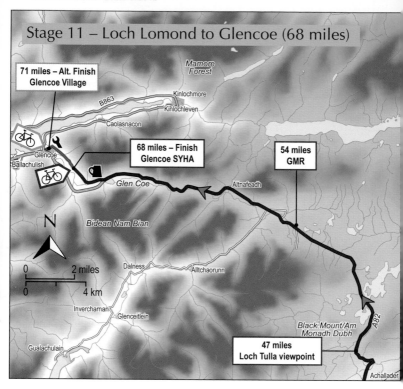

Stage 11 – Loch Lomond to Glencoe (68 miles)

71 miles – Alt. Finish
Glencoe Village

Mamore
Forest

Kinlochmore

B863

Kinlochleven

Caolasnacon

68 miles – Finish
Glencoe SYHA

54 miles
GMR

Glencoe

Ballachulish

Glen Coe

Altnafeadh

N

Bidean Nam Bian

0   2 miles

0   4 km

Dalness

Alltchaorunn

Invercharnan

Glenceitlein

Gualachulain

Black Mount/Am
Monadh Dubh

A82

47 miles
Loch Tulla viewpoint

Achallader

Glen Coe, perhaps Scotland's most visited glen, has been associated with the mighty **Clan Donald** since the 14th century, when Angus Og MacDonald of Islay bestowed the Glencoe lands on his son Iain Fraoch, the ancestor of the Glencoe MacDonalds. By the 17th century, however, the Earls of Argyll were the acknowledged feudal superiors of Glencoe and the MacDonalds paid a high price for their support of the Jacobite Rebellion, at the hands of the Earl of Argyll's regiment at the infamous Massacre of Glencoe in 1692.

The End to End now navigates through 16 miles of some of the most dramatic scenery in all of Scotland. Leave the Loch Tulla viewpoint and continue to follow the A82 for 7 miles. This section can present a challenge; it is over 300m above sea level and exposed to the elements. The weather can change quickly even in

Traditional music at the Loch Tulla viewpoint

summer. If the weather is favourable, there can be few finer views in all of Europe; the Highland panorama is tremendous.

Passing the entrance to **Glencoe Mountain Resort** (NN 267 537) marks the start of the final 9 miles through the Pass of Glen Coe, which is dominated by Buchaille Etive Mor (1022m) and the looming Three Sisters, a trio of buttresses guarding the approach to Bidean nam Bian at 1150m, which can be seen on the left-hand side of the road. Having passed the Three Sisters turn right (NN 138 566) following signs for Glencoe Village and the **Clachaig Inn** public house (NN 128 567; www.clachaig.com; tel: 01855 811252). Continue along this quiet lane for 1 mile to reach **Glencoe Youth Hostel**, Ballachulish PH49 4HX (NN 118 576; www.syha.org.uk; tel: 01855 811219).

Alternative finish

To reach Glencoe Village, continue for a further 1¾ miles to reach B&B or hotel accommodation in the village centre (NN 102 588).

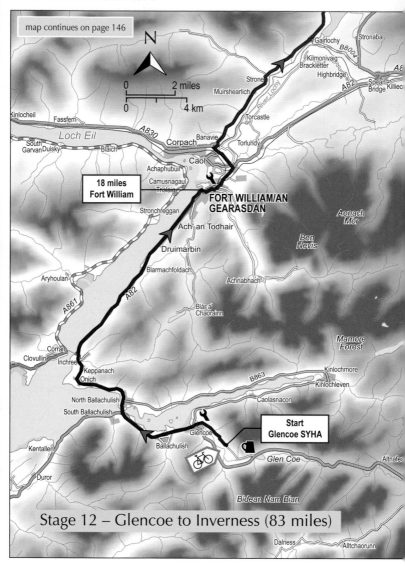

map continues on page 146

N

0   2 miles
0   4 km

Gairlochy   Stronaba
B8004
Kilmonivaig   Brackletter
Stronc   Highbridge   A8
Spean   Killiec
Muirshearlich   Bridge
River Lochy

Kinlocheil   Fassfern   Torcastle
Loch Eil   A830   Banavie
South   Duisky   Blaich   Corpach   Torlundy
Garvan
Caol
Achaphubuil
18 miles   Camusnagaul   Aonach
Fort William   Trislaig   Mór
FORT WILLIAM/AN
Stronchreggan   GEARASDAN
Ach an Todhair   Ben
Nevis
Druimarbin
Blarmachfoldach   Achriabhach
Aryhoulan
A861   A82   Blàr a'
Chaorainn
Mamore
Forest
Corran   Kinlochmore
Clovullin   Inchree   Kinlochleven
Keppanach
Onich   B863   Caolasnacon
North Ballachulish
South Ballachulish   Start
Glencoe SYHA
Glencoe
Kentallen   Ballachulish   Glen Coe   Altnafea
Duror

Bidean Nam Bian

Stage 12 – Glencoe to Inverness (83 miles)

Dalness   Alltchaorunn

144

STAGE 12
Glencoe to Inverness

Start	Glencoe SYHA (NN 118 576)
Finish	Inverness city centre (NH 665 452)
Distance	83 miles (134km)
Grade	Hard
Time	8–9 hours
Maps	OS Landranger 34: Fort Augustus; OS Landranger 26: Inverness & Strathglass area
Refreshments	The Scots Kitchen, Main Street, Fort Augustus; tel: 01320 366 361; www.scotskitchen.com; family-run café and takeaway

This stage of the End to End is visually stunning but long and tough, and involves further cycling on the A82. To the north of Fort William there is a short stretch of excellent forest track cycling and a section on the cycle path running alongside the Caledonian Canal. The second half of the day involves the steepest climb of the entire End to End route to reach General Wade's Military Road above Fort Augustus, followed by superb cycling along high ground to the east of Loch Ness before concluding with an exhilarating descent into the fine city of Inverness.

To get things started on this stage of the End to End leave **Glencoe Youth Hostel** (NN 118 576) and turn left; cycle for 1¾ miles to the junction of the B863 and the A82 (NN 098 587) on the outskirts of Glencoe Village, turn right onto the A82 and follow signs for Fort William A82 and Oban (A828). Remain on the A82 for approximately 16 miles to **Fort William** and follow the A82 northwards towards Inverness. Cycle past Fort William railway station (NN 107 743) and continue for approximately 1½ miles to the junction of the A82 and the A830, turn left following signs for Mallaig onto the A830 (NN 125 758).

Remain on the A830 for approximately 1¼ miles into Banavie, going over the swing bridge spanning the Caledonian Canal, and turn right onto the B8004 (NN 111 769).

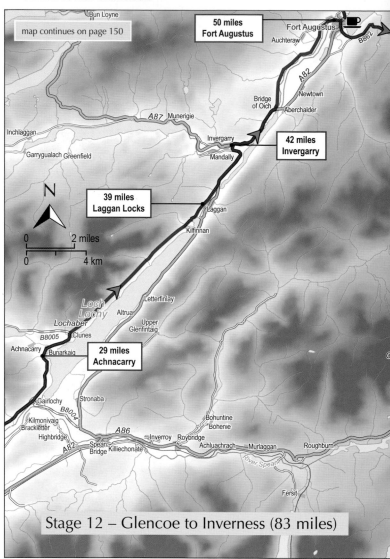

map continues on page 150

Stage 12 – Glencoe to Inverness (83 miles)

THE CALEDONIAN CANAL

A typical stretch of Telford's canal

The Caledonian Canal is a fine example of 19th-century engineering. The origins of its construction lie in the political and economic pressures of the day; in the late 18th century the Highlands had an overpopulation problem – too many people, too little agricultural land – leading to poverty and emigration. The government recognised that these two issues were problematic, not least because the Highlanders were valuable recruits into the military. They also possessed some rudimentary information that public works could have a positive social impact, which, in this instance, could help stem the tide of emigration and alleviate poverty and unemployment.

It was against this backdrop that work on the Caledonian Canal commenced in 1803. The canal was surveyed, designed and built by Thomas Telford at a cost of £900,000, taking nearly two decades to complete before finally opening in October 1822. The canal is 62 miles long and comprises 29 locks, eight of which, known as Neptune's Staircase, can be found close to the swing bridge at Banavie. The canal was designed to be deeper and wider than preceding canals, capable of taking ocean-going vessels, and it cleverly incorporated the natural features of the Great Glen by linking the narrow natural lochs of Lochy, Oich, Ness and Dochfour with 22 miles of man-made canal engineering. Upon completion the canal formed a nexus between the Beauly Firth to the east and the Atlantic to the west, via Loch Linnhe and the Sound of Mull, saving vessels the long, treacherous passage through the Pentland Firth between the northern coast of the Scottish mainland and Orkney. It also allowed fishermen from both the east and west quick access to markets. Today, its halcyon days as a bustling trade route are long over; the canal is now a magnet for pleasure craft, with thousands of vessels using the waterway each year.

Once over the swing bridge at Banavie, cycle along the B8004 for 6 miles to the hamlet of Gairlochy (NN 175 844), and follow the NCN78 towards Fort Augustus. Make sure that you do not take the right fork in the road at the ambiguous junction in Gairlochy. If you descend towards the village and the Caledonian Canal this is the wrong direction. Follow the sign for the Clan Cameron Museum. The B8004 descends to the right and **you should now continue on the B8005**, which is the left fork in the road. The route affords views of the Caledonian Canal and Loch Lochy to the right. After a further 2 miles cycling from Gairlochy the route passes the entrance to the Clan Cameron Museum at **Achnacarry** (NN 184 876; www.clan-cameron.org/museum.html).

The understated entrance to the museum belies the important role that nearby **Achnacarry Castle** (NN 175 880) played in the Second World War. Thousands of British servicemen, along with their comrades from the United States, Holland, Belgium, Poland and Norway, trained in the forests, lochs and cliffs that surround this remote location. These men were undertaking a

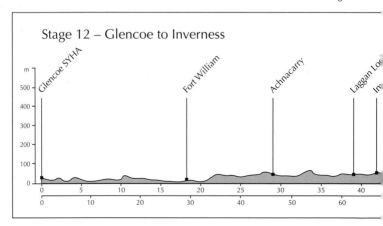

Stage 12 – Glencoe to Inverness

Beside Loch Lochy en route to Fort Augustus

gruelling basic commando course before being sent, firstly to a holding unit, then on to an active service unit. The potential commandos were introduced to the basic training course with a 7-mile speed march from nearby Spean Bridge to Achnacarry. The standards required of the recruits were exceptionally high; any soldier falling short was quickly returned to his unit. The speed

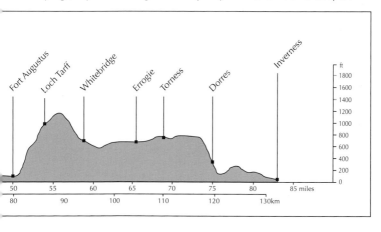

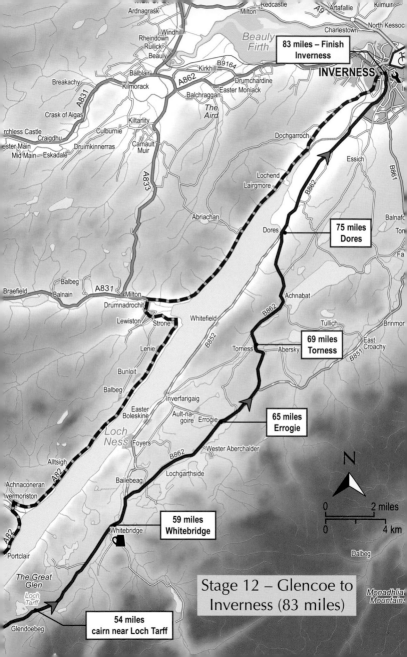

83 miles – Finish
Inverness

INVERNESS

75 miles
Dores

69 miles
Torness

65 miles
Errogie

59 miles
Whitebridge

54 miles
cairn near Loch Tarff

N

0   2 miles
0   4 km

Stage 12 – Glencoe to
Inverness (83 miles)

march from Spean Bridge was a sharp introduction to what was to follow: 40-mile marches conducted over 24 hours, cliff and amphibious assaults, live ammunition exercises and survival training. The basic commando course was designed to make the men mentally and physically tough, supremely fit and willing to have a go at the enemy wherever or whenever they found him.

Continue onwards from the entrance to the Clan Cameron Museum along the B8005 (NCN78) for 1¾ miles to the hamlet of Clunes (NN 201 887), turn right and cycle for a further 7½ miles along the NCN78 route through Clunes Forest, which runs adjacent to Loch Lochy (NN 215 895). You will be leaving the sealed road surface at Clunes. The NCN78 shares the forest track alongside the loch with the famous long-distance walking route, the Great Glen Way. You will find that the NCN78 has a reasonably good, shale-type surface, ideally suited for hybrid and touring bicycles, although road bicycles can navigate the track but will need to use extra care to avoid punctures. The forest route from Clunes towards Laggan is also notable for two steep climbs and a solitary descent. After cycling for approximately 7½ miles the track gives way to tarmac. At the next fork in the road (NN 283 964), look for a sign for the Great Glen Hostel to the left and take the right fork. Cycle on to the small marina at **Laggan Locks**, cross the footbridge spanning the Caledonian Canal, continue for approximately 160m to the junction with the A82 (NN 288 962) and turn left towards Fort Augustus.

Continue on the A82 for approximately 3¾ miles to the village of **Invergarry** (NH 308 011). Follow signs for Inverness and turn right, remaining on the A82. Continue along the A82 for approximately 2½ miles to Aberchalder swing bridge (NH 336 036), turn left into a car park and cycle along the NCN78 canal-side cycle path for 4½ miles to **Fort Augustus** (NH 378 094), passing through Cullochy Lock (NH 341 042) and Kytra Lock (NH 352 068) en route.

Alternative route to Inverness

You now have the option of an alternative, flat route to the capital of the Highlands. This requires turning left onto the A82 and cycling along Loch Ness for 33½ miles to the bustling Highland city. However, the A82 between Fort Augustus and Inverness is notable for numerous tourist coaches as well as articulated lorries carrying wood, both of which ply their trade along the narrow carriageway.

The preferred route to Inverness, although hilly, is quiet and uses the spectacular General Wade's Military Road. To access this highly recommended route, leave the NCN78 by the Caledonian Canal at Fort Augustus, turn right onto the A82 and cycle in the direction of Fort William for approximately 250m, before turning left on the B862 Glendoe Road (NH 379 091) following signs for Whitebridge, Errogie, Dores and Foyers. The next 5¼ miles involve a climb that is guaranteed to live long in the memory, as the road steeply ascends from 33m to 393m above sea level – perhaps the hardest and longest climb of the entire End to End route. The exceptional scenery and lack of heavy traffic make this a hugely rewarding experience. The end of the ascent is marked by a **cairn near Loch Tarff** at 393m (NH 449 105).

Looking north from the cairn you will see the B862 stretching away into the distance as it follows the high ground to the east of Loch Ness, linking Fort Augustus with Inverness. This road is steeped in history, part of a network of four arterial roads built between 1725 and 1733 by **General George Wade** to project the power of the British government deep into the Highlands in the wake of the Jacobite rebellion. The roads were designed to facilitate the movement of men and materiel, yet their construction also sent out a clear message of intent to the rough clansmen: that the Hanoverians were here to stay. The roads were built by soldiers who were paid an extra sixpence a day for their labours; Wade called these men his Highwaymen, with as many as 500 working on a particular stretch of road at any one time. They would spend summer nights sleeping in crude camps close to their work, returning to barracks in winter.

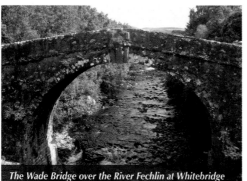

The Wade Bridge over the River Fechlin at Whitebridge

Besides identifying the location of General Wade's Military Road, the cairn also marks the beginning of a 4-mile descent to **Whitebridge** (NH 486 154), with the **Whitebridge Hotel** the last significant navigational waypoint before a 16½-mile ride through exposed heath and moorland on the B862, passing through **Errogie** (NH 556 224) and **Torness** (NH 580 270) before concluding with a sharp and exhilarating descent into the village of **Dores** (NH 599 348). Having arrived in Dores, at the junction of the B852 and B862 turn right towards **Inverness** and continue on the B862 for approximately 8¼ miles into the city centre (NH 665 452), which offers a wide range of accommodation to suit all budgets.

STAGE 13

Inverness to the Crask Inn

Start	Inverness railway station (NH 667 456)
Finish	The Crask Inn, by Lairg (NC 524 247)
Distance	66 miles (106km)
Grade	Moderate/Hard
Time	6–7 hours
Maps	OS Landranger 21: Dornoch & Alness; OS Landranger 16: Lairg & Loch Shin
Refreshments	Cooperative store, Evanton (NH 607 661), snacks and drinks; Spar shop, Lairg (NC 583 065), snacks and drinks

The penultimate leg of the End to End can best be described as brilliant. The navigation is straightforward and the cycling memorable. The day starts with a short stretch of urban cycling out of the city of Inverness, over the Kessock Bridge and mainly through country lanes to Dingwall. There is then a short and steep hill climb out of the town to the nearby village of Evanton. At 24m above sea level, the village signals the start of a gradual but long ascent of nearly 200m onto the Struie. The nearby viewpoint at Cadha Mor offers spectacular views of the Dornoch Firth to the east and the Kyle of Sutherland to the west. The next village is Bonar Bridge, which is a convenient stopping point before a memorable leg through Lairg and on to the solitary Crask Inn.

Today's ride begins at **Inverness** railway station (NH 667 456), easily located on the B865 in Academy Street. To leave Inverness, cycle along Academy Street with the railway station to the right, into Chapel Street and to the roundabout at the junction of Shore Street and Longman Road (NH 664 458). Take the second exit off the roundabout and continue to cycle along Shore Street, following signs for the NCN1 for about a mile as the route winds through the harbour side of Inverness. The NCN1 is well signed as it traverses the city towards the large, unmistakable structure of the Kessock Bridge (NH 665 475), which spans the Moray Firth (to the east) and the **Beauly Firth** (to the west).

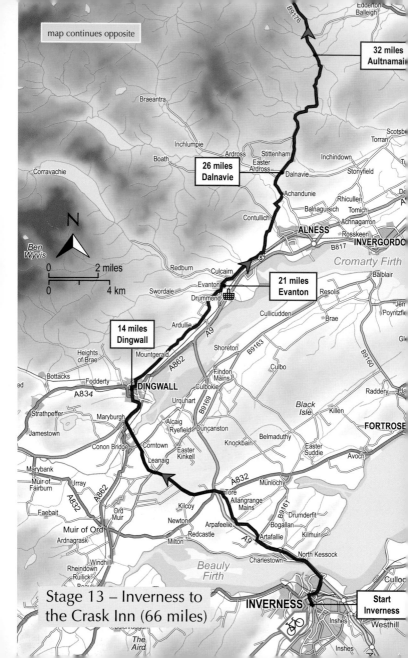

map continues opposite

32 miles Aultnamai...

Braeantra

Inchlumpie

Ardross Stittenham
Boath Easter Inchindown
Ardross
26 miles Dalnavie Dalnavie Stonyfield

Corravachie Achandunie Rhicullen

Balnaguisich Tomich

Contullich Achnagarron

ALNESS Rosskeen **INVERGORDO**
B817

Cromarty Firth

Ben Wyvis Redburn Culcairn Bālblair

Evanton **21 miles Evanton** Resolis
0 | 2 miles
0 | 4 km Swordale Drummond Jerr
Poyntzfie

Cullicudden Brae

Ardullie A9 Gl

14 miles Dingwall Shoreton B9163

Heights Mountgerald A862 Findon Culbo
of Brae Mains B9160
Bottacks Fodderty **DINGWALL** Culbokie Raddery T

A834 Urquhart B9169 Black
Strathpeffer Maryburgh Alcaig Duncanston Isle Killen **FORTROSE**
Jamestown Ryefield
Conon Bridge Corntown Easter Knockbain Easter Avoch
Leanaig Kinkell Belmaduthy Suddie

Marybank A832
Muir of Urray Tore Munlochy
Fairburn A862 Allangrange
Faebait Ord Mains B9161 Drumderfit
Muir Kilcoy
Muir of Ord Newton Arpafeelie Bogallan Kilmuir
Ardnagrask Milton Redcastle A9 Artafallie
North Kessock
Windhill *Beauly* Charlestown Culloc
Rheindown *Firth*
Rüilick **Start Inverness**

Stage 13 – Inverness to **INVERNESS** Westhill
the Crask Inn (66 miles) Inshes

The Aird Inshes

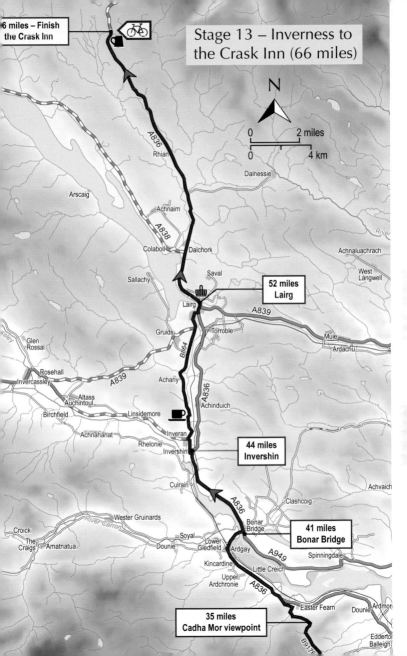

Stage 13 – Inverness to the Crask Inn (66 miles)

N

| 0 | | 2 miles |
| 0 | | 4 km |

66 miles – Finish
the Crask Inn

A836

Rhian

Dalnessie

Arscaig

Achnairn

A838

Colaboll — Dalchork

Achnaluachrach

West
Langwell

Sallachy — Saval

**52 miles
Lairg**

Lairg

A839

Muie
Ardachu

Gruids — Torroble

Glen
Rossal

B864

Rosehall
Invercassley

A839

Achany

Altass
Auchintoul

A836

Birchfield — Linsidemore

Achinduich

Achnahanat

Inveran

Rhelonie

**44 miles
Invershin**

Invershin

Culrain

Achvaich

Wester Gruinards

Clashcoig

River Garron

Croick
The
Craigs — Amatnatua

Soyal

Dounie

Lower
Gledfield
Ardgay

Bonar
Bridge

**41 miles
Bonar Bridge**

A949

Spinningdale

Kincardine

Little Creich

Upper
Ardchronie

A836

Easter Fearn

Ardmor
Dounie

**35 miles
Cadha Mor viewpoint**

Eddertor
Balleigh

B917

The **Kessock Bridge** was officially opened by HM Queen Elizabeth II on 19 July 1982; the 1052m span is the last major architectural structure on the journey north. The bridge was built to improve the transport links to the far north of Scotland in response to the first North Sea oil expansion and was modelled on the 260m Theodor Heuss Bridge over the River Rhine near Dusseldorf. The Kessock Bridge is supported by two sets of steel cables arranged in a harp configuration. The bridge is exposed to strong, consistent winds from the east and more turbulent winds from the west, causing engineering challenges now ameliorated by the installation of eight massive dampers to prevent the bridge from moving in high winds. Not only is the Kessock Bridge an impressive way of crossing the Moray Firth, but the deck is also a place from which wildlife such as bottlenose dolphins and harbour porpoise can sometimes be seen in the waters below.

Having crossed the Kessock Bridge, remain on the NCN1 cycle path, taking care not to use the A9 (T), and follow the NCN1 towards Dingwall and Cromarty. The NCN1 follows a quiet lane running to the north-east of the main A9 (T), and after approximately 4¼ miles from the Kessock Bridge, you should pass the Tore Burial Ground (NH 612 513). Continue for ¾ mile, to the junction with the A832 at Tore (NH 605 525). Turn left at this junction, then go straight over the nearby busy roundabout with the A9, following the NCN1 signed for Conon Bridge and Dingwall. Cycle along the A835 for 2¾ miles and turn right (NH 562 538) following signs for the B9169 to Culbokie, then cycle onwards for approximately 180m and turn left following the NCN1 signs towards Torgorm (NH 563 539). Now cycle along this lane for 1¼ miles; at the junction with the B9163 (NH 552 556) turn left then immediately right onto the A835 and use the cycle path, signed NCN1, to travel towards Dingwall. Continue for a further mile to the roundabout at the junction of the A835 and A862 (NH 544 570). At this roundabout take the third exit signed A862 Dingwall and cycle for a further 1½ miles along a cycle path running alongside the A862 carriageway into the centre of **Dingwall**.

Stage 13 – Inverness to the Crask

156

Stopping to take photos of the Beauly Firth from the Kessock Bridge

Continue into the centre of this small Highland town; at the traffic lights at the junction of the A862 and A834 (NH 548 588) follow the NCN1 and signs for Alness, Tain and Bonar Bridge on the A862. Cycle straight on for approximately ½ mile, passing Tesco and Dingwall Academy. At the traffic lights at the junction of Craig Road and Tulloch Avenue (NH 550 594) turn left following signs for the

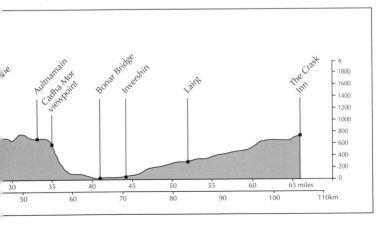

NCN1, Swimming Pool, Sports Centre and Tulloch Castle Hotel. Cycle up Tulloch Avenue for ¼ mile and turn right (NH 549 598) at the top of the hill, into Old Evanton Road, following signs for the NCN1 and the North. Remain on the NCN1 for approximately 5½ miles and cycle into the village of **Evanton**. The **Co-op** (NH 607 661) is a good place to stock up with snacks and drinks before the long and challenging ride over the Struie.

Leave Evanton, cycling along the B817 for approximately 2 miles to the junction with the B9176 (NH 632 682). Turn left here for the start of a 19-mile cycle ride to Bonar Bridge, taking in **Dalnavie** (NH 645 736) and **Aultnamain** (NH 665 814) on the way. The B9176 is known locally as the Struie, a tremendous road with very little traffic; it ascends gradually through grand scenery, passing through patches of forest then dramatic rugged landscape as the road rises to over 200m above sea level. Almost 6 miles before Bonar Bridge, **Cadha Mor viewpoint** (NH 654 858) is a great place to stop and enjoy the Highland scenery. On a clear day there are views of Carbisdale Castle and a number of Sutherland Munros to the north. Having savoured one of the finest vistas in all of Scotland descend for 1¾ miles to the junction with the A836 (NH 634 873) and turn left, continuing onwards for 4 miles into Bonar Bridge (NH 610 915).

Arrival in **Bonar Bridge** is marked by the 38-year-old bridge spanning the Dornoch Firth and the Kyle of Sutherland. Cycle across the bridge and turn immediately left following signs for Lairg. Remain on the A836 and continue for approximately 3¼ miles to the hamlet of **Invershin** (NH 580 954), where you will observe an impressive railway bridge and an integral footbridge leading to Carbisdale Castle SYHA (NH 575 954; Culrain IV24 3DP; tel: 01549 421232).

Cycle on from the railway bridge at Invershin for approximately ¾ mile and

The Bonar Bridge war memorial, with the bridge just visible behind

The Crask Inn – a welcome sight at the end of a long day

turn left signed for Lochinver on the A837 (NH 577 965); this turning is also signed NCN1. After turning left onto the A837 continue for approximately ¾ mile and turn right onto the B864 (NH 574 975); this junction is signed Lairg via Shin Falls B864. Now cycle along the B864 to the **Falls of Shin Visitor Centre** (NH 575 995; www.fallsofshin.co.uk), which is open throughout the year and has a restaurant. Continue for 3¾ miles to the junction of the B864 with the A839 (NC 581 050). At this junction turn right towards Lairg and cycle onwards for approximately ¾ mile to the junction with the A836 (NC 581 060); turn left and cycle into **Lairg (NC 583 065)**. Cycle through the village passing the **Spar** shop on the left; this is the last shop where you can stock up with drinks and snacks before cycling out towards the isolated Crask Inn.

Cycle along the A836 for approximately 2½ miles to the junction of the A838 and A836. At this junction (NC 573 100) go straight on, following signs for Tongue on the A836, and cycle onwards for approximately 9¾ miles to the **Crask Inn** (NC 524 247), one of the finest pubs in the United Kingdom, which has B&B accommodation within the pub itself and a quirky yet comfortable bunk house just across the road. The Crask Inn is situated at 223m above sea level and marks the conclusion of the day's ride.

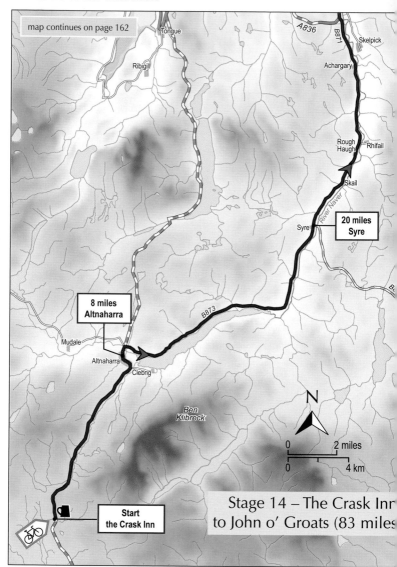

map continues on page 162

Tongue

Ribigill

Skelpick

Achargary

Rough Haugh

Rhifail

Skail

River Naver

20 miles Syre

Syre

8 miles Altnaharra

B873

Mudale

Altnaharra

Clebrig

Ben Klibreck

N

0   2 miles

0   4 km

Start the Crask Inn

Stage 14 – The Crask Inn to John o' Groats (83 miles)

STAGE 14
The Crask Inn to John o' Groats

Start	The Crask Inn, by Lairg (NC 524 247)
Finish	John o' Groats souvenir shop (ND 381 735)
Distance	83 miles (134km)
Grade	Hard
Time	8–9 hours
Maps	OS Landranger 10: Strath Naver; OS Landranger 11: Thurso & Dunbeath; OS Landranger 12: Thurso & Wick
Refreshments	Bettyhill (NC 707 618), shop, drinks and snacks; the Castle Arms (ND 287 727), drinks

The first miles on the final leg between the Crask Inn and Bettyhill provide some of northern Europe's most sensational cycling, on a remarkable stretch of road that could have been designed to the exact specifications of the long-distance cycle tourist. The road undulates gently for miles; the surface is extremely good; there is hardly any traffic; the landscape is breathtaking and the area is steeped in history. Against the backdrop of towering Ben Klibreck, the first hour or so will be spent cycling along Strathnaver, where there is a chance of catching sight of a golden eagle, black grouse or ptarmigan. The character of the ride changes at Bettyhill, where there are some stiff climbs for the first 15 miles along the rugged coastline towards Thurso. If the wind is blowing hard from the east or northeast, then the beauty of the run from the Crask Inn will become a distant memory as you struggle onwards head to wind. However, a fair wind of reasonable strength from the west or south-west will propel you quickly towards Reay, and by the time you arrive in this village you will have completed all of the most strenuous climbs. The remaining miles of the End to End are rather gentle and the navigation is easy, giving time for reflection on what will have been an epic journey.

To start the final day of the End to End, stop for a photograph at the Sustrans marker outside the **Crask Inn** and then cycle onwards for approximately 8 miles to the hamlet of **Altnaharra** (NC 568 353). Go past the Altnaharra Hotel and after approximately ½ mile turn right onto the B873 (NC 569 359) and follow signs for Syre and Bettyhill. These next few miles are sumptuous, with the route following

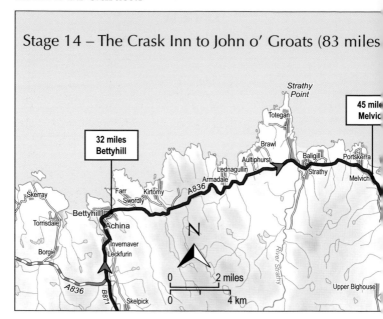

Stage 14 – The Crask Inn to John o' Groats (83 miles

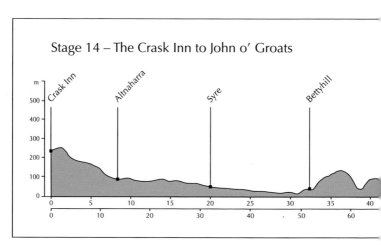

Stage 14 – The Crask Inn to John o' Groats

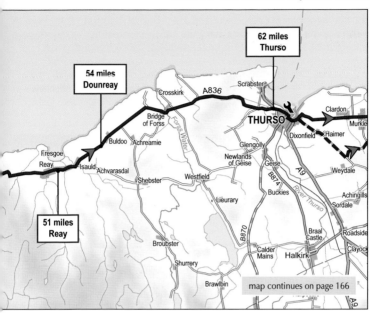

map continues on page 166

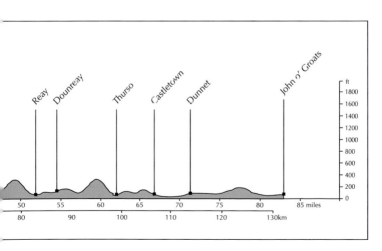

163

the northern bank of Loch Naver and the course of the River Naver towards Bettyhill. After 10 miles cycling along the B873 the dark history of the region is alluded to by a memorial (NC 684 422) on the right-hand side of the road.

Erected in 1980, the memorial marks the memory of Donald Macleod, who witnessed the destruction of the nearby village of Rosal during the **Highland Clearances** – an infamous period of Scottish history largely undertaken in the period between 1770 and 1860.

THE HIGHLAND CLEARANCES

The Clearances were part of the industrial and agricultural revolutions that altered the social and economic landscape of Europe in the late 18th and early 19th centuries.

In common with other places in the Highlands, a key reason for the clearance of Strathnaver lay in the perceived inefficiency of the old communal farming system, which barely returned a profit to the estates of the wealthy landowners. Strathnaver formed part of the huge Sutherland estates owned by Elizabeth, Countess of Sutherland, and the financial benefits of displacing the residents and turning the land over to sheep were irresistible. Communal farmers traditionally kept a few sheep in their townships – animals that were often small and thin, yielding very little wool or mutton. They grazed with the cattle or roamed wild, never strong enough to survive a winter on the hill.

This all changed with the appearance of the 'Great Sheep' – the Cheviot from the south. Hardy enough to withstand the toughest Scottish winter, it was a sheep that provided substantial returns in terms of both wool and mutton – valuable commodities, rising in price due to the demands of the Napoleonic Wars. Elizabeth embarked on an ambitious scheme of 'improvement' and, with the help of her factor, the cruel and efficient Patrick Sellar (a man destined to become the most despised man in the Highlands), hundreds of families were evicted from their homes in Strathnaver and moved to Bettyhill and other villages along the northern coast. Others who were made homeless emigrated, never to return.

By 1822, the upshot of the Strathnaver clearances was that the former population had gone, they were away living on the coast in small two- or three-acre allotments. Their landlord ensured that the size of the land they farmed was never quite enough to sustain them, so they were forced to eke out other ways of adding to their meagre incomes, such as fishing for lobster or herring. Strathnaver was now a series of huge sheep farms.

The 'tin church' at Syre, built as a mission church in 1891 to serve the agricultural community of the Sutherland Estate

From the Strathnaver Clearance Memorial cycle onwards for a further 1½ miles to reach the junction of the B873 and B871 at **Syre**. Here, the distinctive corrugated iron church (NC 694 439) is a useful navigational marker.

From Syre cycle along the B871 for approximately 9¼ miles to the junction with the A836; follow signs for Bettyhill, Melvich and Thurso and continue for approximately 2½ miles to the small community of **Bettyhill**; on the approach to the village there are exceptional views of the white sandy beaches of Torrisdale Bay. Bettyhill (NC 707 618) is a convenient place to stock up with drinks and snacks before pushing on towards Thurso and John o' Groats.

Having left Bettyhill, continue for ½ mile and look out for a former church built in 1774 on the northern side of the A836. The last religious service held in this building was during the Second World War and it is now home to the Strathnaver Museum.

> The **Strathnaver Museum** (Clachan, KW14 7SS; tel: 01641 521418; **www.strathnavermuseum.org.uk**) is open 10.00am–5.00pm from April to October (closed Sunday). It houses some interesting artefacts that focus on local crofting life, the Highland Clearances and Clan Mackay. A few yards to the west of the church stands the 2.3m-tall, lichen-covered Farr Stone (NC 714 622), which marks the grave of an unknown person who must have carried some local political importance. The design of the stone is that of a ringed cross and it is believed to date from around AD800 to 850.

Leave the Strathnaver Museum and remain on the A836 for 13¾ miles to **Melvich**. This is a challenging part of the route as the road ascends and descends following the rugged coastline. Continue for a further ¾ mile and cross the bridge spanning the River Halladale (NC 894 632); remain on the A836 for a further 7½ miles to pass through **Reay** (NC 967 648) and reach the entrance to **Dounreay** Nuclear Power Development Establishment (NC 997 669).

> **Dounreay** provides an interesting and unusual visual contrast to the surrounding Caithness farmland and the Atlantic Ocean to the north. A combination of rectangles, cubes and a large sphere dominate the barren landscape in a visual legacy of the 1960s, when the British government embraced the 'white

heat of technology'. The finest British scientific, engineering and research talent sought to develop nuclear fast breeder technology at this remote location. Between 1958 and 1994 three reactors were operational on the civilian site at Dounreay; today this trio of reactors are all being decommissioned, a process that will take many decades.

Nonetheless, the iconic apple-green sphere remains the most striking building on the site. It enclosed the Dounreay Fast Reactor, which in 1961 became the first fast breeder reactor in the world to supply electricity to a national grid. The sphere was originally designed and built to mitigate the effects of a blast or fire within the reactor; it is now contaminated with low levels of radiation and, like the rest of the site, is destined for demolition, in one of the most complex nuclear demolition projects in the world.

From the entrance to Dounreay cycle onwards on the A836 for a further 7½ miles to the junction with the A9 on the outskirts of Thurso (ND 108 689). Continue on the A9 into **Thurso** for approximately ¾ mile, passing St Andrews Church and the Bank of Scotland (ND 116 685). At the traffic lights close to the Central Hotel turn right into Traill Street and continue for 180m before turning left at the next set of traffic lights onto the A9, Sir George's Street. Signs at this junction (ND 116 684) also indicate the North and West Highlands Route and John o' Groats. Remain on Sir George's Street for ¼ mile, going over the bridge spanning the River Thurso. (At this point, if traffic is busy, you could pick up the alternative route from Thurso to John o' Groats described below and marked with a dashed red line on the maps.)

Turn left onto the A836 following signs for Castletown, John o' Groats and the Castle of Mey. Remain on the A836 for 5 miles to **Castletown** (ND 192 681), then continue for a further 3¼ miles to the turning signed for Dunnet Head (ND 222 713).

If you are not too eager to finish the ride and have a little time there is an interesting 9-mile detour to reach the most northerly point in mainland Britain at **Dunnet Head**, where you will be rewarded with amazing views of sea cliffs and scientifically important coastal grassland. At certain times of the year, Dunnet Head is also home to cormorants, fulmars, kittiwakes, puffins, razorbills and guillemots. To reach Dunnet Head turn left off the A836 in the village of Dunnet (ND 222 713) and take the B855 out to the lighthouse (ND 203 768).

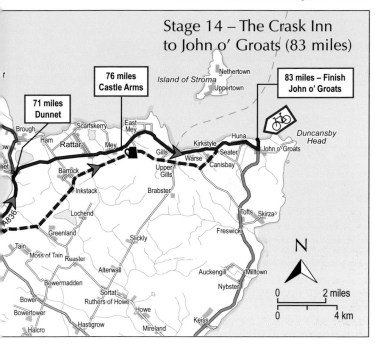

Stage 14 – The Crask Inn
to John o' Groats (83 miles)

71 miles
Dunnet

76 miles
Castle Arms

Island of Stroma

Nethertown

Uppertown

83 miles – Finish
John o' Groats

Brough

Ham

Scarfskerry

East
Mey

Rattar

Mey

Huna

Kirkstyle

Duncansby
Head

Gills

Warse

Seater

John o' Groats

Barrock

Upper
Gills

Canisbay

Inkstack

Brabster

Lochend

Tofts

Skirza

Greenland

Slickly

Freswick

Tain

Moss of Tain

Reaster

Alterwall

Bowermadden

Auckengill

Milltown

N

Bower

Sortat

Ruthers of Howe

Nybster

Bowertower

Howe

Halcro

Hastigrow

Mireland

Keiss

0   2 miles

0   4 km

Having visited the lighthouse return to the hamlet of **Dunnet** via the B855, turn left and cycle on the A836 for another 4½ miles to the **Castle Arms** (ND 287 727; www.castlearms.co.uk, tel: 01847 851244), which is a convenient place for a celebratory dram or even a cup of tea. A ¼ mile beyond is the entrance to the Castle of Mey (ND 290 729), the former residence of Her Majesty Queen Elizabeth the Queen Mother.

The **Castle of Mey** is thought to have been built between 1566 and 1572; its Z-plan design and corbelled turrets are a typical example of 16th-century construction, with gun slits on the ground and first floors. The castle was originally called Barrogill Castle. It was almost in ruins when it was purchased in 1952 by the Queen Mother, who restored the castle and landscaped the gardens. In 1996 she secured the castle's future by bequeathing it to The Queen Mother Castle of Mey Trust. It is possible to visit the castle between 1 May and 30 September (**www.castleofmey.org.uk**; tel: 01847 851473).

Ticking off the final miles

From the entrance to the Castle of Mey only 7 miles remain to the finish; stay on the A836 to the junction of the A836 and A99, an unremarkable yet hugely significant road junction (ND 380 727), distinguished only by the Seaview Hotel. Turn left here onto the A99 for the final ½-mile descent to the finish line at **John o' Groats** (ND 381 735). Months of preparation, two weeks of hard work, nearly 1000 miles of cycling, dozens of hills, numerous left and right turns, roundabouts, ferries, bridges, flyovers and underpasses, and in the blink of an eye it's over; all that remains is to savour the moment, to raise a glass and feel proud at completing the End to End.

Should you finish the End to End after 5.00pm you will probably find that in common with Land's End the iconic distance fingerpost is missing. This thwarts any plans to take souvenir photographs against the backdrop of the Pentland Firth and the Orkney Islands. However there is a marker in front of the souvenir shop, by the harbour wall, which will suffice as proof of completion.

Alternative route from Thurso to John o' Groats

To avoid the A836 east of Thurso and add 1½ miles to the final section of your End to End journey, you can choose to follow the NCN1 towards John o' Groats on lanes to Castletown and Canisbay. This quiet NCN1 alternative route then rejoins the A836 at Seater for the concluding 2¼ miles to the finish. The peaceful route is worth taking, especially on weekdays as the A836 can be particularly busy with workers leaving the Dounreay complex for their homes in Wick and beyond.

After cycling over the bridge that spans the River Thurso, turn left following the signs for Castletown, John o' Groats and the Castle of Mey. After ¼ mile turn right (ND 123 682) onto Mount Pleasant Road. This is the NCN1. Cycle along Mount Pleasant Road for 2½ miles before turning left (ND 155 657) and then continue onwards for 3 miles into **Castletown**. Turn right onto Main Street and continue for 1 mile, then turn right (ND 205 681). Continue on the NCN1 for 4¼ miles, past Loch Heilen on the right, to the hamlet of Inkstack (ND 259 703). From Inkstack cycle on for 6 miles to the village of Canisbay (ND 348 721).

> For many End to Enders the name **John o' Groats** will have cropped up numerous times on training rides, in conversations with friends, family and even strangers. Standing in the vestibule of Canisbay Church is the tombstone of the former ferry operator Jan de Groot, who died on 13 April 1568 – the very man whose name is the origin of what we call John o' Groats. Jan de Groot ran the ferry between the mainland and the Orkney Islands. Canisbay Church is also the most northerly place of worship in mainland Scotland, where the late Queen Mother worshipped when in residence at the Castle of Mey, occupying Castle Pew in the north transept.

From Canisbay continue on the NCN1 to pass John o' Groats SYHA, before rejoining the A836 at Seater and turning right (ND 353 728) for the final 2¼ miles to **John o' Groats**.

John o' Groats and the Pentland Firth

APPENDIX A

Route summary table

Stage	Start	Finish	Distance	Time	Page
1	Land's End Visitor Centre	Fowey town centre or Golant	64 miles (103km) or 67 miles (108km)	6–7 hours	25
2	Bodinnick Ferry, Fowey	Moretonhampstead town centre	55 miles (89km)	5½–6½ hours	37
3	Moretonhampstead town centre	Street or Glastonbury town centre	72 miles (116km) or 74 miles (120km)	7–8 hours	48
4	Street	Monmouth town centre	68 miles (109km)	6½–7½ hours	60
5	Monmouth Tourist Information Centre	Clun village centre	53 miles (85km)	5–6 hours	73
6	Clun village centre	Holiday Inn, Runcorn	80 miles (129km)	8½–9 hours	83
7	Holiday Inn, Runcorn	Hark to Bounty public house, Slaidburn	63 miles (101km)	6½–7½ hours	93
8	Hark to Bounty public house, Slaidburn	Keswick	71 miles (114km)	7½–8½ hours	101
9	Keswick war memorial	Moffat town centre	72 miles (116km)	7½–8½ hours	113
10	Moffat town centre	Loch Lomond or Balloch town centre	85 miles (137km) or 83 miles (134km)	8–9 hours	122
11	Loch Lomond	Glencoe or Glencoe Village	68 miles (109km) or 71 miles (114km)	6½–7½ hours	137
12	Glencoe	Inverness city centre	83 miles (134km)	8–9 hours	145
13	Inverness railway station	The Crask Inn	66 miles (106km)	6–7 hours	153
14	The Crask Inn	John o' Groats	83 miles (134km)	8–9 hours	161

APPENDIX B
OS maps covering the route

The following Ordnance Survey maps in the 1:50,000 Landranger series, listed here in route order, cover the whole End to End route described in this guide. The particular sheets needed for each stage are also identified in the information box at the start of its route description.

203: Land's End & Isles of Scilly
204: Truro & Falmouth
200: Newquay & Bodmin
201: Plymouth & Launceston
191: Okehampton & North Dartmoor
192: Exeter & Sidmouth
193: Taunton & Lyme Regis
182: Weston-super-Mare
172: Bristol & Bath
162: Gloucester & Forest of Dean
149: Hereford & Leominster
137: Church Stretton & Ludlow
126: Shrewsbury & Oswestry
117: Chester & Wrexham
108: Liverpool
109: Manchester
103: Blackburn & Burnley
98: Wensleydale & Upper Wharfedale

97: Kendal & Morecambe
90: Penrith & Keswick
85: Carlisle & Solway Firth
78: Nithsdale & Annadale
71: Lanark & Upper Nithsdale
64: Glasgow
63: Firth of Clyde
56: Loch Lomond & Inveraray
50: Glen Orchy & Loch Etive
41: Ben Nevis
34: Fort Augustus
26: Inverness & Strathglass
21: Dornoch & Alness
16: Lairg & Loch Shin
10: Strath Naver
11: Thurso & Dunbeath
12: Thurso & Wick

APPENDIX C
Accommodation

All information was accurate at the time of going to press in Autumn 2011 but is naturally subject to change.

Land's End

Hostels
Land's End YHA (SW 364 305)
Letcha Vean
St Just in Penwith
Penzance TR19 7NT
tel: 01736 788437 or 0845 371 9643;
email: landsend@yha.org.uk;
www.yha.org.uk.
Fully open between 28 March and 30 October in 2011. Reception hours 8.00am–10.00am and 5.00pm–10.00pm; prices from £16 per person per night

Penzance Backpackers
The Blue Dolphin
Alexandra Road
Penzance TR18 4LZ
tel: 01736 363836;
www.pzbackpack.com;
email: info@pzbackpack.com. Dormitory rooms £16 per person per night. Private rooms £36 per night for two people sharing

YMCA Penzance and Penzance Backpackers
International House
The Orchard, Alverton Street
Penzance TR18 4TE
tel: 01736 365016;
www.ymcacornwall.org.uk
www.cornwallbackpackers.org.uk;
email: penzanceadmin@ymcacornwall.org.uk;
Dormitory bed space £14, single room £18

Hotels
Land's End Hotel
Land's End
Cornwall TR19 7AA
tel: 01736 871844;
www.landsendhotel.co.uk.
2010 tariff B&B April to October £55; May, June and September £60; July and August £70

Whitesands Land's End Hotel
Sennen, near Land's End
TR19 7AR
tel: 01736 871776;
www.whitesandshotel.co.uk.
B&B from £39 per person

Bed and Breakfast
Mayon Farmhouse
Sennen
Penzance TR19 7AD
tel: 01736 871757;
£24–£30 per night; 1½ miles from Land End

Bosavern House
St Just in Penwith
Penzance TR19 7RD
tel: 01736 788301;
www.bosavern.com;
email: info@bosavern.com;
£33–£40 per person per night

Old Success Inn
Sennen TR19 7RD
tel: 01736 871232

Boswedden House
St Just in Penwith TR19 7NJ
tel: 01736 788733

The Commercial
Market Square
St Just in Penwith TR19 7HE
tel: 01736 788455;
www.commercial-hotel.co.uk

Trevore Cottage
Crows-an-Wra
Penzance TR19 6HU
tel: 01736 810370;
www.trevorecottage.co.uk;
email: sheelaghodonnell@btinternet.com;
£30–£38 per person per night

Treeve Moor House
Sennen TR19 7AE
tel: 01736 871284
or mobile: 07771 914660;
email: info@firstandlastcottages.co.uk;
£30–£45 per person per night

Bosvargus Barn
Tregeseal Valley
St Just in Penwith TR 19 7PF
tel: 01736 787356
or mobile: 07811 682201;
www.bosvargusbarn.co.uk;
email: bosvargusbarn@aol.com

Belerion
Treave Barns
Land's End,
Cornwall
Mrs A Benyon, tel: 01736 810343
or mobile: 07754 455484

The Old Fire Station
Nancherrow Terrace
St Just in Penwith TR19 7LA
tel: 01736 786463;
www.oldfirestationstjust.com;
email: enquiries@oldfirestationstjust.com

Sea View House
Porthcurno TR19 6JX

tel: 01736 810638;
www.seaviewhouseporthcurno.com;
email: svhouse@btinternet.com

Lower Treave Farm House
Lower Treave Farm
Crows-an-Wra
Penzance TR19 6HZ
tel: 01736 810100;
email: cromlin@btconnect.com

Myrtle Cottage
Old Coastguard Row
Sennen Cove
Sennen TR19 7BZ
01736 871698

Pengelly House
Sennen Cove
Sennen TR19 7DF
tel: 01736 871866
or mobile: 07810 361739;
email: stay@pengellyhouse.com

Campsites

Trevaylor Caravan and Camping Park
Bottallack
St Just in Penwith
Penzance TR19 7PU
tel: 01736 787016;
email: trevaylor@cornishcamping.co.uk;
1 person 1 tent from £5 (SW 368 325)

Trevedra Farm Caravan and Camping
Sennen
Penzance TR19 7BE
tel: 01736 871818
(SW 369 274)

Caravan and Camping Club
Higher Tregiffian Farm
St Buryan
Penzance TR19 6JB
tel: 01736 871588

Fowey

Hostel
Golant YHA
Penquite House
Golant, Fowey PL23 1LA
tel: 01726 833507;
www.yha.org.uk;
email: golant@yha.org.uk;
this hostel has a restaurant and reception is
open 8.00am–10.00am and 5.00pm–10.30pm.
The hostel closes at 11.00pm. The hostel also
has secure cycle storage.

Hotels
The Cormorant Hotel
Golant, Fowey PL23 1LL
tel: 01726 833426;
www.cormoranthotel.co.uk

The Fowey Hotel
The Esplanade
Fowey PL23 1HX
tel: 01726 832551
(reservations: 0800 005 3904);
www.thefoweyhotel.co.uk; 4 star

Fowey Hall Hotel
Hanson Drive
Fowey PL23 1ET
tel: 01726 833866;
www.foweyhallhotel.co.uk

The Old Quay House Hotel
28 Fore Street
Fowey PL23 1AQ
tel: 01726 833302;
www.theoldquayhouse.com;
email: info@theoldquayhouse.com

Bed and Breakfast
Foye Old Exchange
12 Lostwithiel Street
Fowey PL23 1BD
tel: 01726 833252
or mobile: 07866 974774;

www.foye-old-exchange.co.uk;
email: bandb@foye-old-exchange.co.uk

Fowey Marine Guest House
21–27 Station Road
Fowey PL23 1DF
tel: 01726 833920;
www.foweymarine.com

Hormond House
55 Fore Street
Polruan-by-Fowey PL23 1PH
tel: 01726 870853;
www.hormondhouse.com;
email: bella@chrisbella.demon.co.uk

Reynards Rest
The Mount
Par, near Fowey PL24 2BZ
tel: 01726 815770;
www.reynardsrest.co.uk;
email: carol@reynardsrest.co.uk

Tredudwell Manor
Lanteglos-by-Fowey PL23 1NJ
tel: 01726 870226
or mobile: 07798 651275;
www.tredudwellmanor.co.uk

Sunnybank
43 Polvillion Road
Fowey PL23 1HG
tel: 01726 832350;
www.sunnybankfowey.co.uk;
email: gill@sunnybankfowey.co.uk

Safe Harbour Hotel
58 Lostwithiel Street
Fowey PL23 1BQ
tel: 01726 833379

Bellscat B&B
Golant, Fowey PL23 1LA
tel: 01726 833 404;
www.bellscat.co.uk;
email info@bellscat.co.uk

Brents
19 Station Road
Fowey PL23 1DF
tel: 01726 833592

Austins B&B
51 Vicarage Meadow
Fowey PL23 1EA
tel: 01726 833705

Pendower
11 Park Road
Fowey PL23 1EB
tel: 01726 833559

River View
20 Park Road
Fowey PL23 1ED
tel: 01726 833498

Campsites
Polruan Holidays
Caravanning, Camping and Holiday Homes
Townsend
Polruan-by-Fowey PL23 1QH
www.polruanholidays.co.uk;
email: polholiday@aol.com;
tel: 01726 870263

Penmarlam Caravanning and Camping Park
Bodinnick by Fowey PL23 1LZ
tel: 01726 870088; fax: 01726 870082;
www.penmarlampark.co.uk;
email: info@penmarlampark.co.uk

Polglaze Farm
Fowey PL23 1JZ
tel: 01726 833642;
www.polglaze.co.uk;
email: info@polglaze.co.uk

East Crinnis Camping and Caravan Park
Lantyan
East Crinnis
Par, St Austell PL24 2SQ

tel: 01726 813023;
fax: 01726 813023;
www.crinniscamping.co.uk

Moretonhampstead

Hostels
Sparrowhawk Backpackers Hostel
45 Ford Street
Moretonhampstead TQ13 8LN;
tel: 01647 440318;
www.sparrowhawkbackpackers.co.uk;
email: ali@sparrowhawkbackpackers.co.uk

Hotels
The White Hart Hotel
The Square
Moretonhampstead TQ13 8NQ
tel: 01647 441340;
fax: 01647 441341;
www.whitehartdartmoor.co.uk;
email: enquiries@whitehartdartmoor.co.uk

Bed and Breakfast
Bovey Castle Hotel
Bovey Castle
North Bovey TQ13 8RE
tel: 0844 474 0077;
fax: 01647 445020;
www.boveycastle.com (SX 732 845)

Cookshayes Country Guest House
Court Street
Moretonhampstead TQ13 8LG
tel: 01647 440 374; fax: 01647 440453;
www.cookshayes.co.uk;
email: cookshayes@aol.com

Great Sloncombe Farm
Moretonhampstead TQ13 8QF;
tel: 01647 440595;
www.greatsloncombefarm.co.uk
(SX 737 863)

The Long House B&B
21 Ford Street
Moretonhampstead TQ13 8LN
tel: 01647 440935;
www.longhousebnb.co.uk

Higher Westcott Farm
Westcott
Moretonhampstead TQ13 8SU
tel: 01647 441205;
www.higherwestcottfarm.com;
email: info@higherwestcottfarm.com

The Woodforde
11a Cross Street
Moretonhampstead TQ13 8NL
tel: 01647 440444;
www.thewoodforde.co.uk;
email: info@thewoodforde.co.uk

B&B Plus
20 Pound Street
Moretonhampstead TQ13 8NX
tel: 01647 441299;
www.bedandbreakfastplus.co.uk

Great Wooston Farm
Moretonhampstead TQ13 8QA
tel: 01647 440367;
www.greatwoostonfarm.com;
email: info@greatwoostonfarm.com

The Walled Garden
Mount Pleasant
Moretonhampstead TQ13 8NY
tel: 01647 441353;
www.moretonwalledgarden.co.uk;
email: anne.short@talktalk.net

Moorcote Country Guest House
Chagford Cross
Moretonhampstead TQ13 8LS
tel: 01647 440966;
www.moorcotehouse.co.uk;
email: enquiries@moorcotehouse.co.uk

Great Doccombe Farm
Doccombe
Moretonhampstead TQ13 8SS
tel: 01647 440694;
www.greatdoccombefarm.co.uk;
email: info@greatdoccombefarm.co.uk

Campsites
Woodland Springs Touring Park
Venton
Drewsteignton EX6 6PG
tel: 01647 231695;
www.woodlandsprings.co.uk;
email: enquiries@woodlandsprings.co.uk
(SX 694 912). Campsite located 5½ miles
north west of Moretonhampstead

Street and Glastonbury

Hostels
Street YHA
The Chalet
Ivythorn Hill
Street BA16 OTZ
tel: 0845 371 9143 or 01458 840070;
www.yha.org.uk;
email: street@yha.org.uk;
reception open 8.30am–10.00am and
5.00pm–9.00pm; the hostel closes at 11.00pm

Glastonbury Backpackers
The Crown Hotel
4 Market Place
Glastonbury BA6 9HD
tel: 01458 833353;
www.glastonburybackpackers.com

Hotels
The Wessex Hotel
5–15 High Street
Street, near Glastonbury
Somerset BA16 OEF
tel: 01458 443383;
www.wessexhotel.com;
email: info@wessexhotel.com

Travelodge Glastonbury Hotel
A39 Wirral Park
Glastonbury BA6 9XE
tel: 0871 984 6339; fax: 01458 833642;
www.travelodge.co.uk

Heaphys
16 Market Place
Glastonbury
Somerset
tel: 01458 837935;
www.heaphys.net;
email: info@heaphys.net

Hawthorns Hotel, Bar and Restaurant
8–12 Northload Street
Glastonbury BA6 9JJ
tel: 01458 831255;
www.hawthornshotel.com;
email: enquiries@hawthornshotel.com

Bed and Breakfast

The Birches
13 Housman Road
Street BA16 OSD
tel: 01458 442902

Kasuli B&B
71 Somerton Road
Street BA16 ODN
tel: 01458 442063

Marshalls Elm Farm
Street BA16 OTZ
tel: 01458 442878

Old Orchard House
Middle Brooks
Street BA16 OUT
tel: 01458 442212

Mullions
51 High Street
Street BA16 OEF
tel: 01458 445110;
fax: 01458 442874;

www.mullions51.co.uk;
email: info@mullions51.co.uk

Apple Tree Guest House
27 Bere Lane
Glastonbury BA6 8BD
tel: 01458 830803;
www.appletreeguesthouse.org.uk;
email: contact@appletreeguesthouse.org.uk

The Glastonbury White House
21 Manor Road House
Glastonbury BA6 9DF
tel: 01458 830886;
www.theglastonburywhitehouse.com;
email: carey@theglastonburywhitehouse.com

Spirals B&B
6 Ashwell Lane
Glastonbury BA6 8BG
tel: 01458 830477;
www.thespirals.co.uk;
email: info@thespirals.co.uk

Wearyall Hill House
78 The Roman Way
Glastonbury BA6 8AD
tel: 01458 835510;
www.wearyallhillhouse.co.uk;
email: enquiries@wearyallhillhouse.co.uk

Haydn House
13a Silver Street
Glastonbury BA6 8BS
tel: 01458 834771
or mobile: 07976 437045;
www.hhglastonbury.com;
email: enquiries@hhglastonbury.com

Arimathean Retreat Glastonbury
Arimathean Cottage
59 High Street
Glastonbury BA6 9DS
tel: 01458 830230;
www.arimatheanretreat.ning.com;
email: lisehanne@googlemail.com

Shoe in the Wall
37 Chilkwell Street
Glastonbury BA6 8DE
tel: 01458 832390

Campsite

The Old Oaks Touring Park
Wick Farm
Wick, Glastonbury BA6 8JS
tel: 01458 831437;
www.theoldoaks.co.uk;
email: info@theoldoaks.co.uk
(ST 523 395)

Monmouth

Hostel

St Briavels YHA
Lydney GL15 6RG
tel: 0845 371 9042;
www.yha.org.uk;
email stbriavels@yah.org.uk
(SO 558 045). 8 miles south of Monmouth

Hotel

Queens Head Hotel
1 St James Street
Monmouth NP25 3DL
tel: 01600 712767
or mobile: 07718 964428;
www.queensheadmonmouth.co.uk;
email: enquiries@queensheadmonmouth.co.uk

The Riverside Hotel
Cinderhill Street
Monmouth NP25 5EY
tel: 01600 715577;
fax: 01600 712668;
www.riversidehotelmonmouth.co.uk;
email: info@riversidehotelmonmouth.co.uk

Bed and Breakfast

Bistro Prego
7 Church Street
Monmouth NP25 3BX
tel: 01600 712600;
www.pregomonmouth.co.uk;
email: enquiries@pregomonmouth.co.uk

The Punch House
Agincourt Square
Monmouth NP25 3BT
tel: 01600 713855;
www.sabrain.com;
email: punchhouse@sabrain.com

Berryfield Park B&B
6 Berryfield Park
Osbaston
Monmouth NP25 3DQ
tel: 01600 715375
or mobile: 07891 334257;
www.monmouthbedandbreakfast.com

Casita Alta
15 Toynbee Close
Osbaston
Monmouth NP25 3NU
tel: 01600 713023;
www.monmouthbedandbreakfast.co.uk;
email: bb.allcock@btinternet.com

Myrtle Place Guest House
45 Wonastow Road
Monmouth NP25 5DG
tel: 01600 713773
or mobile: 07984 600112;
www.myrtleplace.co.uk;
email: myrtleplace@googlemail.com

Church Farm Guest House
Mitchel Troy
Monmouth
Gwent NP25 4HZ
tel: 01600 712176;
www.churchfarmmmitcheltroy.com;
email: info@churchfarmguesthouse.eclipse.co.uk

Penylan Farm
The Hendre
Monmouth NP25 5NL
tel: 01600 716 435; fax: 01600 719391;
www.penylanfarm.co.uk;
email: penylanfarm@gmail.com

Old Hendre Farm
Wonastow
Monmouth
Monmouthshire NP25 4DJ
tel: 01600 740447; fax: 01600 740605;
www.oldhendrefarm.co.uk;
email: enquiries@oldhendrefarm.co.uk

Campsite

Glen Trothy Caravan and Camping Park
Mitchel Troy
near Monmouth NP25 4BD
tel: 01600 712295;
www.glentrothy.co.uk
(SO 496 105)

Monmouth Caravan Park
Southfield
Rockfield Road
Monmouth
tel: 01600 714745
(SO 504 126)

Clun

Hostel

Clun YHA
The Mill, Clun
Craven Arms, Shropshire
tel: 0845 371 9112; fax: 0845 371 9127;
www.yha.org.uk;
reception open 8.00am–10.00am and
5.00pm–10.00pm. Hostel closes at 10.00pm.
Cycle storage and camping available. This
hostel is self-catering with a well-equipped
kitchen

Hotel

The Castle Hotel
Bishop's Castle SY9 5BN
tel: 01588 638403;
www.thecastlehotelbishopscastle.co.uk;
email: stay@thecastlehotelbishopscastle.co.uk;
5½ miles from Clun

Bed and Breakfast

The White Horse Inn
The Square, Clun SY7 8JA
tel: 01588 640305;
www.whi-clun.co.uk

Clun Farm House
High Street, Clun
Shropshire SY7 8JB
tel: 01588 640432;
www.clunfarmhouse.co.uk

The Old Farmhouse
Woodside, Clun
Shropshire SY7 0JB
tel: 01588 640695;
www.theoldfarmhousebandb.co.uk;
email: helen@theoldfarmhousebandb.co.uk

Thomas Cottage
Church Bank, Clun
Shropshire SY7 8LP
tel: 01588 640029 or mobile: 07791 953834;
www.thomascottageclun.co.uk

Crown House
The Old Stables and Saddlery
Church Street, Clun SY7 8JW
tel: 01588 640780;
www.crownhouseclun.com;
email: info@crownhouseclun.com

The Sun Inn
10 High Street
Clun SY7 8JB
tel: 01588 640559;
www.thesunatclun.co.uk;
email: info@thesunatclun.co.uk

The Birches Mill
Clun SY7 8NL (SO 285 845)
tel: 01588 640 409;
www.birchesmill.co.uk;
email: birchesmill@btinternet.com

Campsite

The Baron at Bucknell
Chapel Lawn Road
Bucknell SY7 0AH
tel: 01547 530549;
www.baronatbucknell.co.uk;
email: info@baronatbucknell.co.uk;
7¼ miles from Clun

Foxholes Castle Camping
Montgomery Road
Bishops Castle SY9 5HA
tel: 01588 638924;
www.foxholes-castle.co.uk

Runcorn

Hotels

Holiday Inn Hotel Runcorn
Wood Lane
Beechwood
Runcorn WA7 3HA
tel: 0871 942 9070;
www.holidayinn.co.uk

The Old Hall Hotel and Restaurant
Main Street
Frodsham WA6 7AB
tel: 01928 732052;
www.oldhallhotelfrodsham.co.uk

The Heathercliffe Hotel
Manley Road
Frodsham WA6 6HB
tel: 01928 733722;
www.heathercliffe.co.uk;
email: manager@heathercliffe.co.uk

Hotel Campanile Runcorn
Low Lands Road
Runcorn WA7 5TP
tel: 01928 581771;
www.campanile-runcorn.co.uk;
email: runcorn@campanile.com

Bed and Breakfast

Bed and Breakfast
79 Grangemoor
Runcorn WA7 5YB
tel: 01928 771338

Egerton Arms
Bridge Street
Runcorn WA7 1BY
tel: 01928 592194

Fountains B&B
10 High Street
Runcorn WA7 1AU
tel: 01928 569799

Hiraeth Guest House B&B
Stanley Villas
15–16 Greenway Road
Runcorn WA7 4NW
tel: 01928 770954

Slaidburn

Hostel

Kings House YHA
Slaidburn
Clitheroe BB7 3ER
tel: 01200 446656;
email: slaidburn@yha.org.uk;
this is a 30-bed hostel that occupies a former
17th-century coaching inn

Dale House Barn
Slaidburn
near Clitheroe BB7 4TS
tel: 01200 446820;
www.dalehousebarn.co.uk

(SD 734 588), contact Cheryl and Chris.
Bunkhouse accommodation in the stunning
Gisburn Forest. Sleeps up to 14 people
with 2 showers, £10 per person per night.
Approximately 7 miles from Slaidburn

Hotel
Eaves Hall Country Hotel
Eaves Hall Lane
West Bradford
Clitheroe BB7 3JG
tel: 01200 425271;
www.eaveshall.co.uk;
email: reservations@eaveshall.co.uk

Bed and Breakfast
Parkers Arms
Newton in Bowland
near Clitheroe BB7 3DY
tel: 01200 446236;
www.parkersarms.co.uk

Hark to Bounty
Slaidburn
Clitheroe, Lancashire
tel: 01200 446246;
www.harktobounty.co.uk;
email: manager@harktobounty.co.uk;
this pub has seven rooms offering bed and
breakfast

Root Farmhouse B&B
Dunsop Bridge
Clitheroe BB7 3BB
tel: 01200 448214;
www.roothouse.co.uk;
email: info@roothouse.co.uk;
approximately 4¼ miles from Slaidburn
(SD 660 499)

Wood End Farm
Dunsop Bridge
Clitheroe BB7 3BE
tel: 01200 448223; (SD 663 503)
approximately 4 miles from Slaidburn

The Inn at Whitewell
near Clitheroe BB7 3AT
tel: 01200 448222;
www.innatwhitewell.com;
email: reception@innatwhitewell.com;
6¼ miles from Slaidburn (SD 658 469)

Waddington Arms
Waddington
near Clitheroe BB7 3HP
tel: 01200 423262;
www.waddingtonarms.co.uk;
6¾ miles from Slaidburn (SD 729 439)

The Aspinall Arms at Mitton
Mitton
Lancashire
BB7 9PQ
tel: 01254 826223;
www.aspinallarms.co.uk;
email: simon@aspinallarms.co.uk

Campsite
Three Rivers Woodland Park
Eaves Hall lane
West Bradford
Clitheroe BB7 3JG
www.threeriverspark.co.uk;
email: enquiries@threeriverspark.co.uk

Keswick

Hostels
Keswick YHA
Station Road
Keswick CA12 5LH
tel: 01768 772484;
email: keswick@yha.org.uk;
www.yha.org.uk;
(reception open 7.00am–11.00pm, hostel
closes at 11.30pm; 85 beds (NY 267 235)

Derwentwater YHA
Barrow House
Borrowdale
Keswick CA12 5UR

tel: 0845 371 9314;
email: derwentwater@yha.org.uk;
reception open 8.30am–10.30pm;
www.yha.org.uk;
2¼ miles from Keswick, 88 beds
(NY 268 200)

Denton House Independent Hostel
Penrith Road,
Keswick CA12 4JW
tel: 017687 75351;
www.vividevents.co.uk;
email: sales@vividevents.co.uk; 58 beds

Hotels
Keswick Lodge
Main Street
Keswick CA12 5HZ
tel: 017687 74584;
www.keswicklodge.co.uk;
email: relax@keswicklodge.co.uk

Highfield Hotel
The Heads
Keswick CA12 5ER
tel: 017687 72508;
www.highfieldkeswick.co.uk

The Keswick Country House Hotel
Station Road
Keswick CA12 4NQ
tel: 0845 305 2111;
www.thekeswickhotel.co.uk;
email: info@choicehotels.co.uk

Bed and Breakfast
Glendale Guest House
Eskin Street
Keswick CA12 4DH
tel: 017687 73562;
www.glendalekeswick.co.uk;
email: info@glendalekeswick.co.uk

Laurel Bank B&B
Penrith Road
Keswick CA12 4LJ
tel: 017687 73006
or mobile: 07980 000047;
www.laurelbankkeswick.co.uk;
email: info@laurelbankkeswick.co.uk

Honister House
1 Borrowdale Road
Keswick CA12 5DD
tel: 01768 773181;
www.honisterhouse.co.uk;
email: honisterhouse@btconnect.com

Brookfield Guest House
Penrith Road
Keswick CA12 4LJ
tel: 017687 72867;
www.brookfield-keswick.co.uk;
email: info@brookfield-keswick.co.uk

Fell House B&B
28 Stanger Street
Keswick CA12 5JU
tel: 017687 72669;
www.fellhouse.co.uk;
email: info@fellhouse.co.uk

The Edwardene Hotel
26 Southey Street
Keswick CA12 4EF
tel: 017687 73586;
www.edwardenehotel.com

The Grange
Manor Brow
Keswick CA12 4BA
tel: 017687 72500;
www.grangekeswick.com

The Anchorage Guest House
14 Ambleside Road
Keswick CA12 4DL
tel: 017687 72813;
www.anchoragekeswick.co.uk;
email: info@anchoragekeswick.co.uk

Hedgehog Hill Guesthouse
18 Blencathra Street
Keswick CA12 4HP
tel: 017687 80654;
www.hedgehoghill.co.uk

Cumbria House
1 Derwentwater Place
Ambleside Road
Keswick CA12 4DR
tel: 017687 73171;
www.cumbriahouse.co.uk;
email: web@cumbriahouse.co.uk

Camping Barn

Causeway Foot Farm
Naddle
Keswick CA12 4TF
tel: 017687 72290;
www.causewayfoot.co.uk;
email: jackie@causewayfoot.co.uk
(sleeps 16) (NY 294 217)

Campsite

Dale Bottom Farm
St Johns-in-the-Vale
Keswick CA12 4TF
tel: 01768 772176
(NY 294 219)

Burns Farm Caravan and Campsite
St John's-in-the-Vale
Keswick CA12 4RR
tel: 017687 79112;
www.burns-farm.co.uk;
email: linda@burns-farm.co.uk
(NY 305 243)

Moffat

Hostel

The Well Road Centre
Huntly Lodge
Well Road
Moffat DG10 9JT
tel: 01683 221040;
email: ben8363@aol.com

Hotel

The Balmoral Hotel
High Street
Moffat DG10 9DL
tel: 01683 220288;
www.thebalmoralhotelinmoffat.co.uk;
email: pgbalmoral@btconnect.com

Star Hotel
44 High Street
Moffat DG10 9EF
tel: 01683 220156;
www.famousstarhotel.co.uk;
email: enquiries@famousstarhotel.co.uk

Moffat House Hotel
High Street
Moffat DG10 9HL
tel: 01683 220039;
www.moffathouse.co.uk;
email: reception@moffathouse.co.uk

Coxhill B&B
Old Carlisle Road
Moffat DG10 9QN
tel: 01683 220471;
www.moffatbedandbreakfast.co.uk;
email: enquiries@hartfellhouse.co.uk

Hartfell House
Hartfell Crescent
Moffat DG10 9AL
tel: 01683 220153;
www.hartfellhouse.co.uk

Morlich House
Ballplay Road
Moffat DG10 9JU
tel: 01683 220589

Moffat B&B
29 Well Street
Moffat DG10 9DP
tel: 01683 221905;
www.moffatbandb.co.uk;
email: stay@moffatbandb.co.uk

Bridge House
Well Road
Moffat DG10 9J
tel: 01683 220558;
www.bridgehousemoffat.co.uk;
email: info@bridgehousemoffat.co.uk

Buchan Guest House
13 Beechgrove
Moffat DG10 9RS
tel: 01683 220378;
www.buchanguesthouse.co.uk;
email: buchanguesthouse@moffatbroadband.net

Dell-Mar
6 Beechgrove
Moffat DG10 9RS
tel: 01683 220260;
www.dell-mar.co.uk;
email: dell.mar@btinternet.com

The Buccleuch Arms Hotel
High Street
Moffat DG10 9ET
tel: 01683 220003;
www.buccleucharmshotel.com;
email: enquiries@buccleucharmshotel.com

Campsite
Moffat Camping and Caravanning Club Site
Hammerlands
Moffat DG10 9QL
tel: 01683 220436;
www.campingandcaravanningclub.co.uk
(NT 086 046)

Balloch and Loch Lomond

Hostel
Loch Lomond SYHA
Auchendennan
Arden G83 8RA
tel: 01389 850226;
www.syha.org.uk
(NS 368 834)

Hotel
The Lomond Park Hotel
Balloch Road
Balloch G83 8SR
tel: 01389 752494;
www.lomondparkcomplex.com

The Waterhouse Inn Hotel
The Square
Balloch Road
Balloch G83 8LE
tel: 01389 752120;
www.waterhouseinn.co.uk

Bed and Breakfast
Internet information for many of the following
B&Bs is available at
www.goscot.co.uk
(click on South Park, Accommodation, Bed
and Breakfast, Balloch)

Tigh-na-Roune
Mollanbowie Road
Balloch
Loch Lomond G83 8EJ
tel: 01389 755547;
email: info@tigh-na-roune.co.uk

Tullichewan Farm
Upper Stoneymollan Road
Balloch G83 8QY
tel: 01389 711190;
email: info@tullichewanfarm.co.uk

Albannach
274 Main Street
Alexandria by Balloch G83 0NU
tel: 01389 603345;
email: enquiries@albannachonline.co.uk

Anchorage Guest House
Balloch Road
Balloch G83 8SS
tel: 01389 753336;
email: anchorage_gh@hotmail.com

Norwood Guest House
60 Balloch Road
Balloch G83 8LE
tel: 01389 750309;
email: norwoodgh@aol.com

Braeburn Cottage
West Auchencarroch Farm
Auchencarroch Road
Balloch G83 9LU
tel: 01389 710998;
email: info@braeburncottage.co.uk

Barton B&B
12 Balloch Road
Balloch G83 8SR
tel: 01389 759653;
email: bartonbandb@yahoo.co.uk

The Tullie Inn
Balloch Road
Balloch
Loch Lomond G83 8SW
tel: 01389 752052

Oakvale
Drymen Road
Balloch G83 8JY
tel: 01389 751615

Monday Cottage
29 Torrinch Drive
Balloch G83 8JL
tel: 01389 759932
Woodvale
Drymen Road
Balloch G83 8HT
tel: 01389 755771

Campsite
Luss Camping and Caravanning Club
Luss, Loch Lomond
near Glasgow G83 8NT
tel: 01436 860658;
www.campingandcaravanningclub.co.uk;
8½ miles from Balloch (NS 360 936)

Glencoe

Hostel
Glencoe Independent Hostel
Glencoe
near Ballachulish PH49 4HX
tel: 01855 811906;
www.glencoehostel.co.uk;
email: info@glencoehostel.co.uk;
42 beds (NN 117 577)

Glencoe SYHA
Glencoe
Ballachulish PH49 4HX
tel: 01855 811219;
www.syha.org.uk;
56 beds (NN 118 576)

Hotel
Kings House Hotel
Glencoe PH49 4HY
tel: 01855 851259;
www.kingy.com
(NN 259 547)

The Glencoe Hotel
Glencoe Village
PH49 4HW
tel: 01855 811245;
www.theglencoehotel.com;
email: info@theglencoehotel.com

Bed and Breakfast

Clachaig Inn
Glencoe
Argyll PH 49 4HX
tel: 01855 811252;
www.clachaig.com

An Darag B&B
Upper Carnoch
Glencoe PH49 4HU
tel: 01855 811643;
www.bedandbreakfastglencoe.co.uk;
email: info@bedandbreakfastglencoe.co.uk

Ardno House B&B
Lettermore
Ballachulish near Glencoe PH49 4JD
tel: 01855 811830;
www.ardnohouse.co.uk;
email: alanyoung3822@btinternet.com

Morven Cottage
Glencoe
Ballachulish PH49 4HS
tel: 01855 811544;
www.morvenbnb.com;
email: enquiries@morvenbnb.com

Scorrybreac Guest House
Glencoe PH49 4HT
tel: 01855 811354;
www.scorrybreacglencoe.com;
email: info@scorrybreac.co.uk

Craiglinnhe House
Lettermore
Ballachulish PH49 4JD

tel: 01855 811270;
www.craiglinnhe.co.uk;
email: info@craiglinnhe.co.uk

Ballachulish Hotel
Ballachulish
Argyll PH49 4JY
tel: 0844 855 9133;
www.ballachulishhotel.com;
email: reservations.ballachulish@
akkeronhotels.com

Campsite

Red Squirrel Campsite
Glencoe
PH49 4HX
tel: 01855 811256;
www.redsquirrelcampsite.com;
email: squirrels@amserves.net
(NN 119 574)

Inverness

Hostel

Highlander Hostel
23a High Street
Inverness IV1 1HY
tel: 01463 221225;
www.highlanderhostel.com;
email: highlanderhostel@highlanderhostel.com

BazPackers Hostel
4 Culduthel Road
Inverness IV2 4AB
tel: 01463 717663;
www.bazpackershostel.co.uk

Inverness SYHA
Victoria Drive
Inverness IV2 3QB
tel: 01463 231771;
www.syha.org.uk;
185 beds

Inverness Tourist Hostel
21 Rose Street
Inverness IV1 1NU
tel: 01463 241962;
www.invernesshostel.com;
email: info@invernesshostel.com

Hotel

The Kingsmills Hotel
Culcabock Road
Inverness IV2 3LP
tel: 01463 237166;
www.kingsmillshotel.com;
email: info@kingsmillshotel.com

Thistle Inverness
Milburn Road
Inverness IV2 3TR
tel: 0871 376 9023;
www.thistle.com

Ramada Inverness
Church Street
Inverness IV1 1QY
tel: 0844 815 9006;
www.ramadajarvis.co.uk

Best Western Palace Hotel and Spa
8 Ness Walk
Inverness IV3 5NG
tel: 01463 223243;
www.invernesspalacehotel.co.uk

Bed and Breakfast

Kiloran Guest House
29 Kenneth Street
Inverness IV3 5DW
tel: 01463 230276;
www.kiloran-of-inverness.com;
email: info@kiloran-of-inverness.com

Trafford Bank Guest House
96 Fairfield Road
Inverness IV3 5LL

tel: 01463 241414;
www.traffordbankguesthouse.co.uk;
email: enquiries@
invernesshotelaccommodation.co.uk

Rossmount Guest House
32 Argyle Street
Inverness IV2 3BB
tel: 01463 229749;
www.rossmount-inverness.com;
email: webmaster@rossmount.co.uk

The Alexander
16 Ness Bank
Inverness IV2 4SF
tel: 01463 231151;
www.thealexander.net;
email: info@thealexander.net

Lyndon Guest House
50 Telford Street
Inverness IV3 5LE
tel: 01463 232551;
www.invernessbedandbreakfast.com;
email: lyndon@invernessbedandbreakfast.com

An Grianan B&B
11 Crown Drive
Inverness IV2 3NN
tel: 01463 250530 mobile: 07765 322494;
www.angrianan.co.uk;
email: telmac@hotmail.co.uk

Avalon Guest House
79 Glenurquhart Road
Inverness IV3 5PB
tel: 01463 239075;
www.inverness-loch-ness.co.uk;
email avalon@inverness-loch-ness.co.uk

Eildon Guest House
29 Old Edinburgh Road
Inverness IV2 3HJ
tel: 01463 231969;
www.eildonguesthouse.co.uk

Royston Guest House
16 Millburn Road
Inverness IV2 3PS
tel: 01463 231243;
www.roystonguesthouse.com;
email: roystonguesthouse@btinternet.com

Campsite
Bught Park Caravan and Campsite
Bught Lane
Inverness IV3 5SR
tel: 01463 236920;
www.invernesscaravanpark.com;
email: bookings@invernesscaravanpark.com;
80 tent pitches (NH 657 439)

Bunchrew Caravan Park
Bunchrew
Inverness IV3 8TD
tel: 01463 237802;
www.bunchrew-caravanpark.co.uk;
125 pitches (NH 618 459)

The Crask Inn
Hostel, Bunk House opposite the Crask Inn
by Lairg IV27 4AB
tel: 01549 411241
(plus B&B within the Crask Inn)

Hotel
Altnaharra Hotel
Altnaharra
by Lairg IV27 4UF
tel: 01549 411222; fax: 01549 411233;
www.altnaharra.com;
email: office@altnaharra.co.uk

Lairg Highland Hotel
Main Street
Lairg IV27 4DB
tel: 01549 402243; fax: 01549 402593;
www.highland-hotel.co.uk;
email: info@highland-hotel.co.uk

The Overscaig House Hotel
Loch Shin
Sutherland IV27 4NY
tel: 01549 431203; fax: 01549 431210;
www.overscaighotel.co.uk;
email: enquiries@overscaig.com.
Closed between October and April

Bed and Breakfast
Park House
Station Road, Lairg IV27 4AU
tel: 01549 402208; fax: 01549 402593;
www.parkhousesporting.com;
email: david-walker@park-house.freeserve.co.uk

Ambleside
Lochside, Lairg IV27 4EG
tel: 01549 402130;
www.amblesidelairg.co.uk

Lochview
Lochside
Lairg IV27 4EH
tel: 01549 402578;
www.lochviewlairg.co.uk;
email: georgemorgan@lochviewlairg.fsnet.co.uk

Altnaharra B&B
1 Macleod Crescent
Altnaharra
Lairg IV27 4UG
tel: 01549 411258;
www.altnaharra.net;
email: info@altnaharra.net

The Bettyhill Hotel
Bettyhill KW14 7SP
tel: 01641 521352
(during 2011 the hotel was being refurbished)

The Farr Bay Inn
Bettyhill
KW14 7SZ
tel: 01641 521230;
www.farrbayinn.co.uk;
email: info@farrbayinn.co.uk

Campsite

Craigdhu Caravan Site
Carlton Miniott
Bettyhill
Thurso KW14 7SP
tel: 01641 521273;
(NC 709 619) open from April to October; 90
pitches, tents £10 per night. Secure bicycle
storage can be arranged with campsite owner

John o' Groats

Hostel

John o' Groats SYHA
Canisbay
near Wick
KW1 4YH
tel: 01955 611761;
open from 30 April to 12 September (20 beds)
(ND 349 722)

Hotel

Seaview Hotel
John o' Groats
Caithness KW1 4YR
tel: 01955 611220;
www.seaviewjohnogroats.co.uk;
open all year

Bed and Breakfast

John o'Groats Guest House
The Broo
John o' Groats
Wick
Caithness KW1 4YR
tel: 01955 611251;
www.johnogroatsguesthouse.co.uk;
email: grant.alistair@talk21.com
(ND 377 729)

Mill House
John o' Groats
Caithness KW1 4YR
tel: 01955 611239

Bencorragh House
Upper Gills
Canisby, by John o' Groats
Caithness KW1 4YD
tel/fax: 01955 611449;
www.bencorraghhouse.com;
email: bartonsandy@hotmail.co.uk

John o' Groats B&B
Hamnavoe – Roadside
John o' Groats
Caithness KW1 4YR
tel: 01955 611776;
www.johnogroatsbnb.com

Campsite

John o' Groats Caravan & Campsite
John o' Groats
Caithness KW1 4YR
tel: 01955 611329
(ND 382 733)

APPENDIX D

Tourist information

General Planning

Visit England
1 Palace Street
London SW1E 5HX
tel: 0207 578 1400;
www.enjoyengland.com;
email: info@enjoyengland.com

Visit Wales
Welsh Assembly Government
Brunel House, 2 Fitzalan Road
Cardiff CF24 0UY
tel: 08708 300306
www.visitwales.co.uk;
email: info@visitwales.co.uk

Visit Scotland
Ocean Point One, 94 Ocean Drive
Edinburgh EH6 6JH
tel: 0845 22 55 121;
www.visitscotland.com;
email: info@visitscotland.com

Stage 1

Visit Cornwall
Pydar House
Pydar Street, Truro
Cornwall TR1 1EA
tel: 01872 322900;
www.visitcornwall.com;
email: enquiries@visitcornwall.com

Visit West Cornwall
www.visit-westcornwall.com

Penzance
Station Approach
Penzance TR18 2NF

tel: 01736 362207;
www.purelypenzance.co.uk;
email: penzancetic@cornwall.gov.uk

St Just
St Just Library
Market Square, St Just TR19 7HX
tel: 01736 788165;
email: stjust.library@cornwall.gov.uk

Fowey
5 South Street, Fowey
Cornwall PL23 1AR
tel: 01726 833616; fax: 01726 834939;
www.fowey.co.uk;
email: info@fowey.co.uk

Stage 2

Heart of Devon Tourism Partnership
Economy and Tourism
Civic Centre, Paris Street
Exeter EX1 1JJ
tel: 01392 265209
www.heartofdevon.com

Dartmoor Partnership Limited
Unit 6 Okehampton Business Centre
Higher Stockley Mead
Okehampton
Devon EX20 1FJ
tel: 01837 52200;
www.discoverdartmoor.com

Moretonhampstead
10–11 The Square
Moretonhampstead TQ13 8NF
tel: 01647 440 043;
www.moretonhampstead.com;
email: moretonvic@yahoo.co.uk

Stage 3

Visit Somerset
Somerset County Council
County Hall, Taunton
Somerset TA1 4DY
tel: 01934 750833
www.visitsomerset.co.uk;
email: tourism@somerset.gov.uk

Glastonbury
9 High Street, Glastonbury
Somerset BA6 9DP
tel: 01458 832954;
www.glastonburytic.co.uk;
email: info@glastonburytic.co.uk

Glastonbury Online
www.glastonbury.co.uk;
tel: 01458 831686

Bristol
E Shed, 1 Canons Road
Bristol BS1 5TX
tel: 0906 711 2191;
www.visitbristol.co.uk;
email: ticharbourside@destinationbristol.co.uk

Stage 4

**Herefordshire and the
Wye Valley Tourist Information**
1 King Street
Hereford HR4 9BW
tel: 01432 268430;
www.visitherefordshire.co.uk;
email: tourism@visitherefordshire.co.uk

**Royal Forest of Dean,
Herefordshire and Monmouthshire**
110 High Street, Broadway
Worcestershire WR12 7AJ
tel: 01386 853790;
www.royalforestofdean.info;
email: webmaster@royalforestofdean.info

Monmouth
Market Hall
Priory Street, Monmouth
Gwent NP25 3XA
tel: 01600 713899;
www.monmouth.org.uk;
email: monmouth.tic@monmouthshire.gov.uk

Stage 5

Shropshire
www.shropshiretourism.co.uk

Stage 6

Cheshire
www.visitcheshire.com

Stage 7

Clitheroe
Visitor Information Centre
Ribble Valley Borough Council
Church Walk, Clitheroe BB7 2RA
tel: 01200 425566;
www.visitribblevalley.co.uk;
email: tourism@ribblevalley.gov.uk

Lancashire
www.visitlancashire.com

Stage 8

Lake District
www.southlakeland.gov.uk
www.lake-district.com
www.visitcumbria.com
www.lakedistrict.gov.uk
www.lakedistricttouristguide.com
www.independenthostelguide.co.uk
www.lakedistrictcamping.co.uk
www.lakedistrict-stay.co.uk
www.discoverthelakes.co.uk
www.explorelakedistrict.co.uk

Keswick
Moot Hall, Main Street
Keswick CA12 5JS
tel: 017687 72645;
www.keswick.org;
email: keswicktic@lake-district.gov.uk

Stage 9

Carlisle
The Old Town Hall
Green Market, Carlisle
Cumbria CA3 8JE
tel: 01228 625600;
www.discovercarlisle.co.uk;
email: tourism@carlisle.gov.uk

Dumfries and Galloway
www.visitdumfriesandgalloway.co.uk

Moffat
Churchgate, Moffat DG10 9EG
tel: 01683 220620;
www.visitmoffat.co.uk;
email: moffat@visitscotland.com

Stage 10

Glasgow and Clyde Valley Tourist Board
11 George Square, Glasgow G2 1DY
tel: 0141 566 0800;
www.seeglasgow.com;
email: accommodation@seeglasgow.com.

Loch Lomond
www.visitscottishheartlands.com
www.loch-lomond.net
www.visit-lochlomond.com
www.lochlomond-trossachs.org

**Loch Lomond, Helensburgh
and West Dunbartonshire**
Balloch Road, Balloch G83 8LQ
tel: 08707 200607;
www.visit-balloch.com;
email balloch@visitscotland.com

Stage 11

Discover Glencoe
www.discoverglencoe.com

The National Trust for Scotland (Glencoe)
www.glencoe-nts.org.uk

**Ballachulish Visitor Centre
and Tourist Information**
Ballachulish PH49 4JB
tel: 01855 811866;
www.glencoetourism.co.uk;
email: info@glencoetourism.co.uk

Stage 12

Fort William
www.visit-fortwilliam.co.uk
www.outdoorcapital.co.uk

Inverness
Castle Wynd, Inverness IV2 3BJ
tel: 08452 255121;
www.visithighlands.com;
email: inverness@visitscotland.com

Welcome Inverness
www.inverness-scotland.com

Stage 13

The Highlands
www.visithighlands.com

Stage 14

Caithness
www.caithness.org

Thurso
Riverside, Thurso KW14 8BU
tel: 018452 255121;
www.visithighlands.com

APPENDIX E
Cycle repair shops en route

Stage 1

Penzance
The Cycle Centre
1 New Street
Penzance TR18 2LZ
tel: 01736 351671;
www.cornwallcyclecentre.co.uk;
email: enquiries@cornwallcyclecentre.co.uk

Halfords
Heliport Link Road
Penzance TR18 3RG
tel: 01736 335910;
www.halfords.com

St Austell
Halfords
Pentewan Road
St Austell PL25 5BU
tel: 01726 68981;
www.halfords.com

Stage 2

Torpoint
Cycle Action
1a Harvey Street
Torpoint PL11 2BU
tel: 01752 815571

Plymouth
Plymouth Cycle Scene
Hyde Park House
Mutley Plain, Plymouth
Devon PL4 6LF
tel: 01752 257701;
www.plymouthcyclescene.co.uk;
email: info@plymouthcyclescene.co.uk

Natural Cycles
Benbow Street, Stoke
Plymouth PL2 1AF
tel: 01752 550729;
www.naturalcycles.co.uk

Certini Bicycle Store
40 Royal Parade
Plymouth PL1 1DY
tel: 01752 267502;
www.certini.co.uk;
email: contact@certini.co.uk

Stage 3

Exeter
Bike Shed
163 Fore Street
Exeter EX4 3AT
tel: 01392 426191;
www.bikesheduk.com

Sidwell Cycles
140–141 Sidwell Street
Exeter EX4 6RT
tel: 01392 272929;
www.sidwellcycles.co.uk

Richards Bikes
145 Pinhoe Road
Exeter EX4 7HY
tel: 01392 279688;
www.richardsbikes.co.uk

Street
On Your Bike
128A High Street
Street BA16 OER
tel: 01458 443048

Stage 4

Wells
Bike City
The Old Chapel Bakery
Union Street
Wells BA5 2PU
tel: 01749 670002;
www.bikecity.biz;
email: info@bikecity.biz

Halfords
Westfield Road
Wells BA5 2HS
tel: 01749 685170;
www.halfords.com

Bristol
Evans Cycles Bristol
Lewins Mead
Bristol BS1 2PY
tel: 0117 927 7639;
www.evanscycles.com

Strada Cycles
236 North Street
Southville
Bristol BS3 1JD
tel: 0117 966 9662;
www.stradacycles.co.uk

Blackboy Hill Cycles
180 Whiteladies Road
Clifton
Bristol BS8 2XU
tel: 0117 9731420;
www.blackboycycles.co.uk

Psyclewerx
4–6 Abbotsford Road, Redland
Bristol BS6 6HB
tel: 0117 946 7946;
www.psyclewerx.co.uk;
email: info@psyclewerx.co.uk

Fred Baker Cycles
144 Cheltenham Road
Bristol BS6 5RL
tel: 0117 924 9610;
www.fredbakercycles.co.uk

Chepstow
559 Bikes
4 Manor Way
Chepstow NP16 5HZ
tel: 01291 626126;
www.559bikes.com

Stage 5

Monmouth
Bridge Cycles of Monmouth
9–13 St Thomas's Square
Monmouth NP25 5ES
tel: 01600 719942;
www.bridgecycles.co.uk;
email: shop@bridgecycles.co.uk

Hereford
Climb On Bikes
24–25 Coningsby Street
Hereford HR1 2DY
tel: 01432 261211;
www.climbonbikes.co.uk;
email: climbonbikes@aol.com

Mastercraft Cycles
39 Bridge Street
Hereford HR4 9DG
tel: 01432 274047;
www.mastercraftcycles.co.uk

Coombes
94 Widemarsh Street
Hereford HR4 9HG
tel: 01432 354373;
www.coombescycles.co.uk

Chaingang Cycles
Unit 10, Marshall Business Centre
Faraday Road
Hereford HR4 9NS
tel: 01432 264449;
www.chaingangcycles.co.uk

Stage 6

Shrewsbury

Stan Jones Cycles
17a Hill Lane
Shrewsbury SY1 1QU;
tel: 01743 343775;
www.stanjonescycles.co.uk;
email: info@stanjonescycles.co.uk

Dave Mellor Cycles
9a New Street, Frankwell
Shrewsbury SY3 8JN
tel: 01743 366662;
www.davemellorcycles.com;
email: sales@thecycleshop.co.uk

Shrewsbury Cycles
43 Ditherington Road
Shrewsbury SY1 4BE
tel: 01743 232061;
www.shrewsburycycles.co.uk

Frodsham
Twelve 50 Bikes
102 Main Street
Frodsham WA6 7AR
tel: 01928 898011;
www.twelve50bikes.com;
email: info@twelve50bikes.com

Stage 7

Warrington

Cyclehouse
Unit 1 Portland Trade Park
Buckley Street
Warrington WA2 7NS
tel: 01925 576555;
www.cyclehouse.co.uk

D & M Cycles
2 Hood Lane
Sankey Bridges
Warrington WA5 1EJ
tel: 01925 653606;
www.dandmcycles.com;
email: p.allman@btconnect.com

MJ Cycles
752 Knutsford Road
Latchford
Warringon WA4 1JS
tel: 01925 650100;
www.mjcycles.com

Leigh

Whittles Cycles
30–32 Leigh Road
Leigh WN7 1RX
tel: 01942 674410

Halfords
1 Parsonage Retail Park
Leigh WN7 5SJ
tel: 01942 677795;
www.halfords.com

Ratcliffes Cyclelife
113A Bradshawgate
Leigh WN7 4ND
tel: 01942 673 481

Bolton

MK Cycles
95/97 Tonge Moor Road
Bolton BL2 2DL
tel: 01204 412762;
www.mkcycles.com;
email: sales@mkcycles.com

Blackburn

Ewood Bikes
178 Bolton Road
Blackburn BB2 4HL
tel: 01254 55515;
www.ewoodbikes.co.uk;
email: ewoodbikes@gmail.com

On Yer Bike Cycles
491–501 Whalley New Road
Blackburn BB1 9AU
tel: 01254 662440;
www.onyerbikeonline.com;
email: info@onyerbikeonline.com

Clitheroe

Pedal Power
17 Waddington Road
Clitheroe BB7 2HJ
tel: 01200 422066;
www.pedalpowerclitheroe.co.uk

Stage 8

Kendal

Evans Cycles
113 Stricklandgate
Kendal LA9 4RF
tel: 01539 740087;
www.evanscycles.com

Staveley

Wheelbase
Mill Yard, Staveley
Kendal LA8 9LR
tel: 01539 821443;
www.wheelbase.co.uk;
email: info@wheelbase.co.uk

Ambleside

Biketreks
Rydal Road
Ambleside LA22 9AN
tel: 01539 431245;
www.bike-treks.co.uk;
email: info@biketreks.net

Stage 9

Keswick

Keswick Bikes Workshop
Southey Hill Industrial Estate
Keswick CA12 5ND
tel: 017687 74407;
www.keswickbikes.co.uk;
email office@keswickbikes.co.uk

Whinlatter Bikes
82 Main Street
Keswick CA12 5DX
tel: 017687 73940;
www.whinlatterbikes.com;
email: shop@whinlatterbikes.com

Carlisle

Scotby Cycles
The Bike Shop
Church Street
Caldewgate
Carlisle CA2 5TL
tel: 01228 546931;
www.scotbycycles.co.uk

Push Bikes UK
155 Botchergate
Carlisle CA1 1SG
tel: 01288 513909;
www.pushbikes-uk.com

Palace Cycles
120–124 Botchergate
Carlisle CA1 1SH
tel: 01228 523142;
www.palacecycles.co.uk

Stage 10

Glasgow

Gear Bikes
19 Gibson Street
Hillhead, West End
Glasgow G12 8NU
tel: 0141 339 1179;
www.gearbikes.com;
email: sales@gearbikes.com;
twitter: @gerabikes

Billy Bilsland
176 Saltmarket
Glasgow G1 5LA
tel: 0141 552 0841;
www.billybilslandcycles.co.uk;
email: sales@billybilslandcycles.co.uk

Alpine Bikes Glasgow (St George's Cross)
6 St George's Place
Glasgow G20 7PW
tel: 0141 353 2226;
www.alpinebikes.com;
email: glasgow@alpinebikes.co.uk

Halfords
9 Rutherglen Road
Glasgow G73 1SX
tel: 0141 647 4911;
www.halfords.com

Dales Cycles Workshop
150 Dobbies Loan
Glasgow G4 0JE
tel: 0141 332 2705;
www.dalescyclesworkshop.co.uk;
email: workshop@dalescycles.com

Philip Lang Cycles
163 Gallowgate
Glasgow G1 5ED
tel: 0141 552 5103;
www.philiplangcycles.co.uk

Bowling

Magic Cycles
Arch 4, Bowling Harbour
Bowling G60 5AF
tel: 01389 873433;
www.magiccycles.co.uk;
email: info@magiccycles.com

Stage 11

Glencoe

Davy Gunn
CrankitUpGear
20 Lorn Drive
Glencoe, Argyll
tel: 01855 811694
or mobile: 0774 686 0023;
www.crankitupgear.com;
email: crankitupgear@aol.co.uk;
twitter: @crankitupgear

Stage 12

Fort William

Nevis Cycles
4–6 Lochy Crescent, Inverlochy
Fort William PH33 6NG
tel: 01397 705555;
www.neviscycles.com;
email: ben@neviscycles.com

Alpine Bikes
117 High Street
Fort William PH33 6DG
tel: 01397 704008,
www.alpinebikes.com;
email: fort_william@alpinebikes.co.uk

Stage 13

Inverness

Highland Bicycle Company
38/40 Waterloo Place
Inverness IV1 1NB
tel: 01463 234789;
www.highlandbikes.com;
email: info@highlandbikes.com; open
Monday to Saturday 9.00am–5.30pm

Monsterbike
7 Canal Road
by Muirtown lock gates
Inverness IV3 8NF
tel: 01463 729500
or mobile: 07752 102700;
www.monsterbikeshop.com;
email: sales@monsterbikeshop.com; open
Monday to Saturday 10.00am–6.00pm and
Sunday 10.00am–4.00pm. Will box bikes
with a day's notice.

Bikes of Inverness
39/41 Grant Street
Inverness IV3 6BP
tel: 01463 225965;
www.bikesofinverness.co.uk;
email: sales@bikesofinverness.co.uk; open
Monday to Friday 9.00am–5.30pm and
Saturday 9.00am–5.00pm. This company will
box bikes ready for flights for £25.

Stage 14

Thurso

Caithness Cycle repairs
tel: 07740 341399; mobile repair service
covering Caithness and northern Sutherland;
contact: Marc MacDonald;
www.caithnesscyclerepairs.co.uk;
email: caithnesscyclerepairs@yahoo.co.uk

The Bike Shop
35 High Street, Thurso
Caithness KW14 8AZ
tel: 01847 895385;
contact: Sean. A well-equipped bike shop that
will also supply bike boxes (£15) for shipping.
Once packed, boxes can be taken to the Post
Office, Meadow Lane, Thurso KW14 8ER (tel:
01847 892044) for onward dispatch.

APPENDIX F
Other useful resources

Cycling apps

GPX files for each stage of the main route, compatible with GPS devices and smartphones, are available to download from the Cicerone website when you register your purchase of *The End to End Cycle Route*. See page 203 for full details. The grid references for the route are also provided in Appendix G.

Bike maintenance
- Bikedoctor – bicycle repairs *from* www.bikedoctorapp.com
- Bike Gears – all the ratios you could possibly need! *from* www.bikegearsapp.com
- Bike Repair – bicycle repairs *from* www.bikerepairapp.com

Trip data
- Bikehub – journey planner *from* www.bikehub.co.uk
- Cyclemeter – time, distance, speed and averages *from* www.abvio.com
- iMapMyRIDE – trip data plus training log/workout features *from* www.mapmyride.com
- MotionX – journey planner and data *from* www.motionx.com

General
- Cychosis – cycling journal *from* www.cychosis.com

Accommodation apps

- AA Bed and Breakfast Guide 2011 *from* www.theaa.com
- Call A Hotel *from* www.ondemandworld.com
- Hotels *from* www.superbreak.com

Websites
- www.aukweb.net
  Audax Long-Distance Cycling Association
- www.britishcycling.org.uk
  National governing body for cycling in the UK
- www.ctc.org.uk
  Cyclists' Touring Club, membership and campaigning organisation
- www.cycle-aid.co.uk
  Specialist cycling lawyers
- www.metoffice.gov.uk
  UK weather forecasts
- www.ordnancesurvey.co.uk
  Ordnance Survey mapping
- www.sustrans.org.uk
  Sustainable transport charity, responsible for the National Cycle Network

Commercial companies offering supported End to Ends
- www.bikeadventures.co.uk
- www.cyclingholidays.org
- www.peak-tours.com
- www.skedaddle.co.uk

Recommended bike shops
- www.cyclesense.co.uk
- www.keeppedalling.co.uk
- www.edinburghbicycle.com
- www.jejamescycles.co.uk
- www.planet-x-bikes.co.uk

APPENDIX G
OS Grid References

Listed below are Ordnance Survey grid references to the core End to End route, slight detours from the route to accommodation points such as Golant YHA and Clun YHA have not been included, to avoid confusion. Other detours to places of interest such as Muchelney Abbey and Dunnet Head are not included for similar reasons; riders should refer to the individual stages for more detailed information. The OS references listed below follow the direct route to John o' Groats from the Land's End Visitor Centre.

Stage 1
(SW 364 305 – Letcha
Vean YHA)
SW 345 250
SW 356 255
SW 395 276
SW 475 305
SW 517 307
SW 534 306
SW 604 344
SW 636 356
SW 661 349
SW 663 347
SW 678 340
SW 678 330
SW 694 334
SW 715 343
SW 727 342
SW 735 366
SW 755 385
SW 781 398
SW 800 404
SW 818 399
SW 841 396
SW 851 392
SW 872 394
SW 903 399
SW 924 423
SW 922 447
SW 955 474
SW 957 474
SW 964 498
SX 025 521

SX 051 531
SX 075 536
SX 088 535
SX 095 529
SX 110 525
SX 125 516

Stage 2
SX 125 516
SX 128 521
SX 135 526
SX 138 528
SX 144 525
SX 156 522
SX 163 523
SX 171 523
SX 181 525
SX 185 531
SX 200 525
SX 206 526
SX 213 531
SX 218 533
SX 254 536
SX 254 542
SX 289 577
SX 335 573
SX 441 551
SX 451 552
SX 454 555
SX 460 555
SX 521 679
SX 591 735
SX 606 749

SX 611 750
SX 649 789
SX 674 809
SX 754 860

Stage 3
SX 754 860
SX 814 888
SX 894 915
SX 914 919
SX 928 933
SX 942 935
SX 956 938
SX 964 944
SX 974 956
SX 984 964
SX 990 969
SX 992 972
SX 998 976
SY 041 978
SY 058 987
SY 065 991
SY 068 992
SY 068 996
SY 074 995
ST 072 029
ST 075 034
ST 089 037
ST 102 048
ST 109 052
ST 116 051
ST 149 056
ST 197 105

ST 203 121
ST 213 126
ST 226 130
ST 235 134
ST 228 151
ST 229 163
ST 232 194
ST 237 215
ST 242 223
ST 244 223
ST 256 227
ST 264 223
ST 265 224
ST 282 230
ST 285 228
ST 394 253
ST 421 267
ST 422 272
ST 489 288
ST 496 288
ST 494 305
ST 490 327
ST 485 344
ST 481 345

Stage 4
ST 481 345
ST 486 374
ST 511 406
ST 514 413
ST 525 417
ST 545 425
ST 549 431

ST 555 436
ST 563 445
ST 545 452
ST 550 464
ST 549 464
ST 552 491
ST 550 502
ST 553 568
ST 556 577
ST 555 594
ST 562 621
ST 562 634
ST 542 648
ST 533 672
ST 530 680
ST 522 691
ST 522 694
ST 522 697
ST 554 713
ST 564 718
ST 564 726
ST 569 721
ST 565 732
ST 523 773
ST 516 785
ST 572 891
ST 569 894
ST 560 901
ST 526 931
ST 524 945
ST 522 968
SO 533 000
SO 535 098
SO 508 129

Stage 5
SO 508 129
SO 510 131
SO 496 199
SO 495 244
SO 493 302
SO 495 324
SO 495 344
SO 495 352
SO 498 355
SO 496 372
SO 505 377

SO 507 395
SO 507 398
SO 507 401
SO 493 406
SO 490 423
SO 463 488
SO 440 570
SO 425 636
SO 425 655
SO 414 690
SO 402 710
SO 398 716
SO 392 726
SO 358 728
SO 356 736
SO 355 740
SO 324 761
SO 320 762
SO 327 770
SO 321 786
SO 315 792
SO 311 801
SO 300 805

Stage 6
SO 300 805
SO 326 884
SO 335 910
SO 333 918
SO 327 996
SJ 350 016
SJ 375 050
SJ 402 060
SJ 458 106
SJ 489 127
SJ 493 135
SJ 475 175
SJ 476 184
SJ 474 198
SJ 472 208
SJ 475 229
SJ 472 239
SJ 472 295
SJ 479 299
SJ 484 302
SJ 463 335
SJ 462 361

SJ 462 372
SJ 464 375
SJ 455 398
SJ 455 401
SJ 458 413
SJ 440 448
SJ 439 455
SJ 435 465
SJ 438 492
SJ 422 540
SJ 423 595
SJ 437 606
SJ 442 618
SJ 453 638
SJ 452 640
SJ 457 644
SJ 456 671
SJ 450 684
SJ 445 696
SJ 474 731
SJ 488 757
SJ 517 779
SJ 530 785
SJ 535 789
SJ 538 796

Stage 7
SJ 538 796
SJ 574 814
SJ 605 861
SJ 604 862
SJ 607 876
SJ 608 879
SJ 612 886
SJ 625 891
SJ 620 898
SJ 643 910
SJ 649 917
SJ 651 930
SJ 652 936
SJ 656 953
SJ 669 983
SJ 670 996
SD 657 000
SD 664 024
SD 659 030
SD 657 057

SD 655 057
SD 663 066
SD 674 086
SD 674 093
SD 681 101
SD 675 110
SD 694 141
SD 674 163
SD 665 185
SD 664 190
SD 664 234
SD 665 243
SD 672 259
SD 676 264
SD 682 274
SD 686 284
SD 705 343
SD 708 348
SD 727 358
SD 734 359
SD 734 365
SD 726 366
SD 716 387
SD 715 390
SD 713 396
SD 709 404
SD 696 426
SD 696 432
SD 672 454
SD 672 457
SD 702 498
SD 696 504
SD 712 524

Stage 8
SD 712 524
SD 712 525
SD 703 590
SD 683 608
SD 668 693
SD 650 694
SD 617 699
SD 603 676
SD 586 679
SD 585 684
SD 584 692
SD 571 699

SD 559 706
SD 558 707
SD 526 731
SD 521 729
SD 521 737
SD 530 765
SD 536 824
SD 524 903
SD 518 916
SD 515 926
SD 497 946
SD 477 973
SD 470 984
SD 460 984
SD 410 988
NY 404 003
NY 376 045
NY 342 070
NY 327 117
NY 325 129
NY 317 140
NY 309 189
NY 316 195
NY 294 219
NY 267 235

Stage 9
NY 267 235
NY 268 234
NY 263 237
NY 261 239
NY 264 244
NY 235 306
NY 250 324
NY 253 330
NY 258 351
NY 268 378
NY 287 385
NY 316 415
NY 369 504
NY 395 561
NY 402 564
NY 395 599
NY 393 646
NY 388 645
NY 383 661
NY 380 685

NY 378 689
NY 346 678
NY 329 681
NY 278 705
NY 193 745
NY 190 748
NY 133 815
NY 101 921
NT 078 029
NT 084 055

Stage 10
NT 084 055
NT 084 056
NT 065 085
NT 035 112
NS 958 186
NS 932 234
NS 928 246
NS 856 326
NS 851 338
NS 848 348
NS 845 350
NS 819 394
NS 812 414
NS 795 432
NS 762 513
NS 751 531
NS 742 543
NS 727 553
NS 722 553
NS 645 605
NS 645 613
NS 600 640
NS 599 642
NS 569 654
NS 568 653
NS 564 658
NS 501 703
NS 465 726
NS 451 735
NS 415 747
NS 397 755
NS 393 754
NS 368 816
NS 381 815
NS 368 834

Stage 11
NS 368 834
NS 373 834
NS 359 846
NN 319 045
NN 317 155
NN 384 251
NN 330 304
NN 325 306
NN 298 396
NN 308 452
NN 267 537
NN 138 566
NN 128 567
NN 118 576
(alt: NN 102 588)

Stage 12
NN 118 576
NN 098 587
NN 107 743
NN 125 758
NN 111 769
NN 175 844
NN 184 876
NN 175 880
NN 201 887
NN 215 895
NN 283 964
NN 288 962
NH 308 011
NH 336 036
NH 378 094
NH 341 042
NH 352 068
NH 379 091
NH 449 105
NH 486 154
NH 556 224
NH 580 270
NH 599 348
NH 665 452

Stage 13
NH 665 452
NH 667 456
NH 664 458

NH 665 475
NH 612 513
NH 605 525
NH 562 538
NH 563 539
NH 552 556
NH 544 570
NH 548 588
NH 550 594
NH 549 598
NH 607 661
NH 632 682
NH 645 736
NH 665 814
NH 654 858
NH 634 873
NH 610 915
NH 580 954
NH 575 954
NH 577 965
NH 574 975
NH 575 995
NC 581 050
NC 581 060
NC 583 065
NC 573 100
NC 524 247

Stage 14
NC 524 247
NC 568 353
NC 569 359
NC 684 422
NC 694 439
NC 707 618
NC 894 632
NC 967 648
NC 997 669
ND 108 689
ND 116 685
ND 116 684
ND 192 681
ND 222 713
ND 287 727
ND 290 729
ND 380 727
ND 381 735

DOWNLOAD THE ROUTE
IN GPX FORMAT

The route of the End to End Cycle Route is available for download from:

www.cicerone.co.uk/EndtoEnd

There are 14 GPX files, one for each of the 14 stages described, which you should be able to load into most formats of mobile device, whether GPS or smartphone.

When you go to this link, you will be asked for your email address and where you purchased the guide, and have the option to subscribe to the Cicerone e-newsletter.

www.cicerone.co.uk

LISTING OF CICERONE GUIDES

The Cathar Way
The GR5 Trail
The Robert Louis Stevenson Trail
Tour of the Oisans: The GR54
Tour of the Queyras
Tour of the Vanoise
Trekking in the Vosges and Jura
Vanoise Ski Touring
Walking in Provence
Walking in the Cathar Region
Walking in the Cevennes
Walking in the Dordogne
Walking in the Haute Savoie North & South
Walking in the Languedoc
Walking in the Tarentaise and Beaufortain Alps
Walking on Corsica

GERMANY

Germany's Romantic Road
Walking in the Bavarian Alps
Walking in the Harz Mountains
Walking the River Rhine Trail

HIMALAYA

Annapurna: A Trekker's Guide
Bhutan
Everest: A Trekker's Guide
Garhwal and Kumaon: A Trekker's and Visitor's Guide
Kangchenjunga: A Trekker's Guide
Langtang with Gosainkund and Helambu: A Trekker's Guide
Manaslu: A Trekker's Guide
The Mount Kailash Trek

IRELAND

Irish Coastal Walks
The Irish Coast to Coast Walk
The Mountains of Ireland

ITALY

Gran Paradiso
Italy's Sibillini National Park
Shorter Walks in the Dolomites
Through the Italian Alps
Trekking in the Apennines
Trekking in the Dolomites
Via Ferratas of the Italian Dolomites: Vols 1 & 2
Walking in Abruzzo
Walking in Sardinia
Walking in Sicily
Walking in the Central Italian Alps
Walking in the Dolomites
Walking in Tuscany
Walking on the Amalfi Coast

MEDITERRANEAN

Jordan – Walks, Treks, Caves, Climbs and Canyons
The Ala Dag
The High Mountains of Crete
The Mountains of Greece
Treks and Climbs in Wadi Rum, Jordan
Walking in Malta
Western Crete

NORTH AMERICA

British Columbia
The Grand Canyon
The John Muir Trail
The Pacific Crest Trail

SOUTH AMERICA

Aconcagua and the Southern Andes
Hiking and Biking Peru's Inca Trails
Torres del Paine

SCANDINAVIA

Trekking in Greenland
Walking in Norway

SLOVENIA, CROATIA AND MONTENEGRO

The Julian Alps of Slovenia
The Mountains of Montenegro
Trekking in Slovenia
Walking in Croatia

SPAIN AND PORTUGAL

Costa Blanca Walks 1 West & 2 East
Mountain Walking in Southern Catalunya
The Mountains of Central Spain
Trekking through Mallorca
Walking in Madeira
Walking in Mallorca
Walking in the Algarve
Walking in the Canary Islands 2 East
Walking in the Cordillera Cantabrica
Walking in the Sierra Nevada
Walking on La Gomera and El Hierro
Walking on La Palma
Walking on Tenerife
Walking the GR7 in Andalucia
Walks and Climbs in the Picos de Europa

SWITZERLAND

Alpine Pass Route
Central Switzerland
The Bernese Alps
Tour of the Jungfrau Region
Walking in the Valais
Walking in Ticino
Walks in the Engadine

TECHNIQUES

Geocaching in the UK
Indoor Climbing
Lightweight Camping
Map and Compass
Mountain Weather
Moveable Feasts
Outdoor Photography
Rock Climbing
Sport Climbing
The Book of the Bivvy
The Hillwalker's Guide to Mountaineering
The Hillwalker's Manual

MINI GUIDES

Avalanche!
Navigating with a GPS
Navigation
Pocket First Aid and Wilderness Medicine
Snow

For full information on all our guides, and to order books and eBooks, visit our website: **www.cicerone.co.uk**.

Walking – Trekking – Mountaineering – Climbing – Cycling

Over 40 years, Cicerone have built up an outstanding collection of 300 guides, inspiring all sorts of amazing adventures.

 Every guide comes from extensive exploration and research by our expert authors, all with a passion for their subjects. They are frequently praised, endorsed and used by clubs, instructors and outdoor organisations.

All our titles can now be bought as **e-books** and many as iPad and Kindle files and we will continue to make all our guides available for these and many other devices.

Our website shows any **new information** we've received since a book was published. Please do let us know if you find anything has changed, so that we can pass on the latest details. On our **website** you'll also find some great ideas and lots of information, including sample chapters, contents lists, reviews, articles and a photo gallery.

It's easy to keep in touch with what's going on at Cicerone, by getting our monthly **free e-newsletter**, which is full of offers, competitions, up-to-date information and topical articles. You can subscribe on our home page and also follow us on **Facebook** and **Twitter**, as well as our **blog**.

Cicerone – the very best guides for exploring the world.

CICERONE

2 Police Square Milnthorpe Cumbria LA7 7PY
Tel: 015395 62069 info@cicerone.co.uk
www.cicerone.co.uk